PIANO • VOCAL • GUITAR

# The Big Book of Love & Wedding Songs

This publication is not for sale in
the E.C. and/or Australia
or New Zealand.

ISBN 0-7935-1440-1

## HAL•LEONARD® CORPORATION

7777 W. BLUEMOUND RD. P.O. BOX 13819 MILWAUKEE, WI 53213

# Contents

# AIR
## (from Water Music Suite)

G. F. HANDEL

Slowly and stately

# ALL I ASK OF YOU
## (From "THE PHANTOM OF THE OPERA")

Music by ANDREW LLOYD WEBBER
Lyrics by CHARLES HART
Additional Lyrics by RICHARD STILGOE

No more talk of dark-ness, for-get these wide-eyed fears; I'm

here, noth-ing can harm you, my words will warm and calm you.

Let me be your free-dom, let day-light dry your tears; I'm

here, with you, be-side you, to guard you and to guide you.

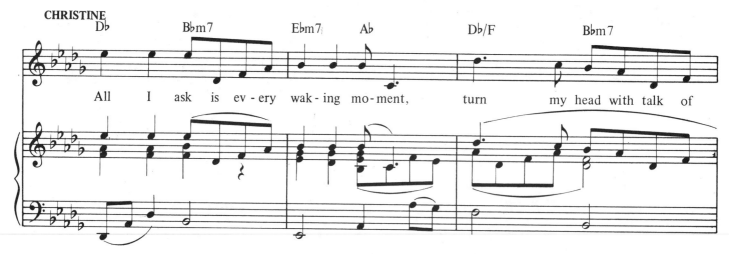

**CHRISTINE**

All I ask is ev-ery wak-ing mo-ment, turn my head with talk of

sum-mer-time. _ Say you need me with you now and al-ways;

pro-mise me that all you say is true, that's all I ask of

Let me be your shel-ter, let me be your light; you're safe, no one will find you, your
you.

fears are far be-hind you. All I want is free-dom, a world with no more night; and

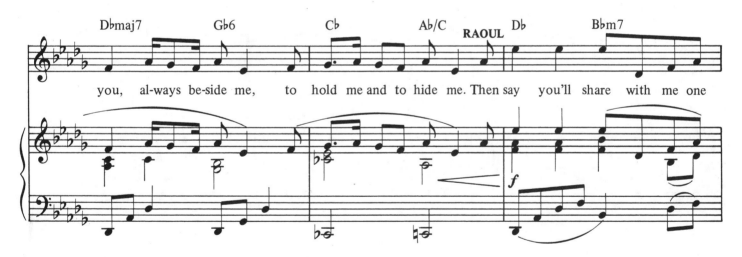

you, al-ways be-side me, to hold me and to hide me. Then say you'll share with me one

love, one life-time; let me lead you from your so-li - tude.

Say you need me with you, here be - side you, an - y where you go, let me go

*rit.* *molto rit.* *a tempo*

CHRISTINE

too, Christ-ine, __ that's all I ask of All I ask for is one

love, one life-time; say the word and I will fol-low you. __

RAOUL

TOGETHER CHRISTINE

Share each day with me, each night, each morn-ing. Say you love me!

You know I

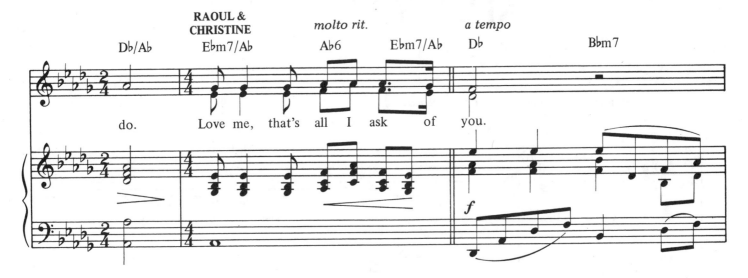

**RAOUL & CHRISTINE**

do. Love me, that's all I ask of you.

*largo*

**CHRISTINE & RAOUL**

An-y-where you go, let me go

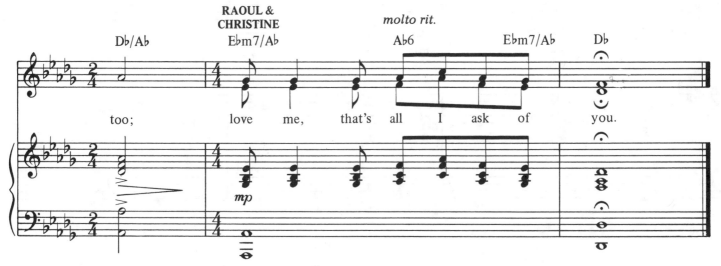

**RAOUL & CHRISTINE**

too; love me, that's all I ask of you.

# ALL MY LOVING

Words and Music by
JOHN LENNON and PAUL McCARTNEY

Brightly, with a swing feel

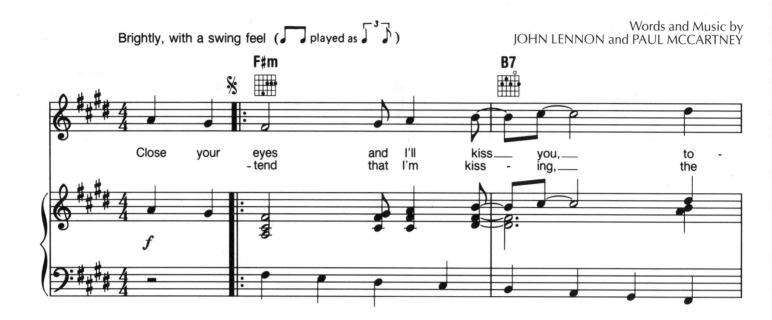

Close your eyes and I'll kiss you, to-
-tend that I'm kiss-ing, to the

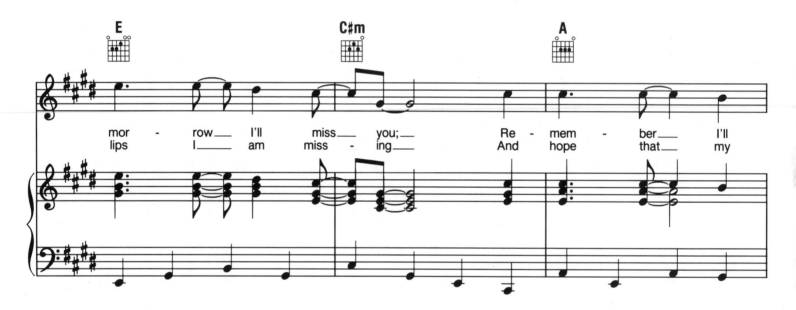

mor-row I'll miss you; Re-mem-ber I'll
lips I am miss-ing And hope that my

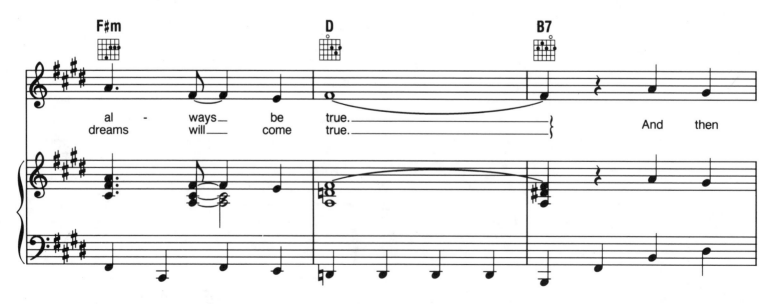

al-ways be true.
dreams will come true. And then

MCA music publishing

you,_____ All___ my lov - ing,___ dar -

- ling, I'll___ be true._____

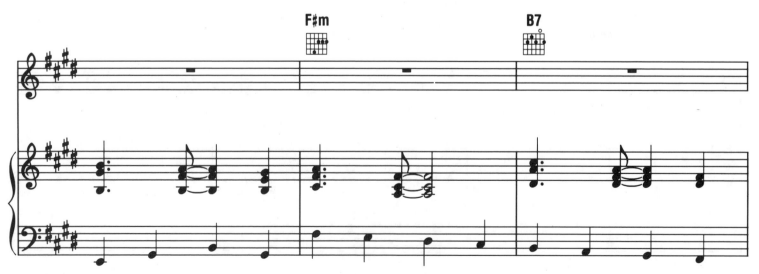

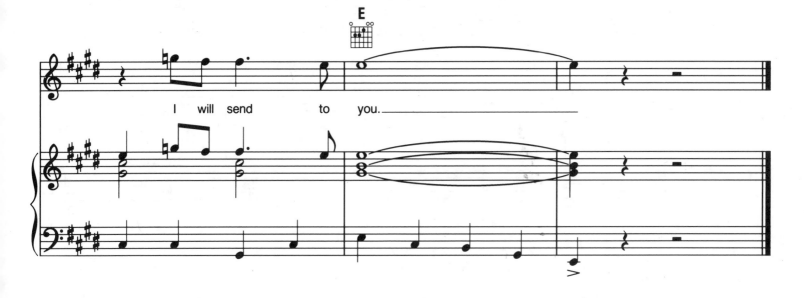

# ALL THE THINGS YOU ARE

## (From "VERY WARM FOR MAY")

Words by OSCAR HAMMERSTEIN II
Music by JEROME KERN

Moderately Slowly

You are the prom - ised kiss of spring - time That

makes the lone - ly win - ter seem long. _____

You are the breath - less hush of eve - ning That

trem - bles on the brink of a love - ly song. _____

_____ You are the an - gel glow _____ that light a

star, _____ The dear - est things I know _____

_____ are what you are. _____

# AND I LOVE HER

Words and Music by
JOHN LENNON and PAUL McCARTNEY

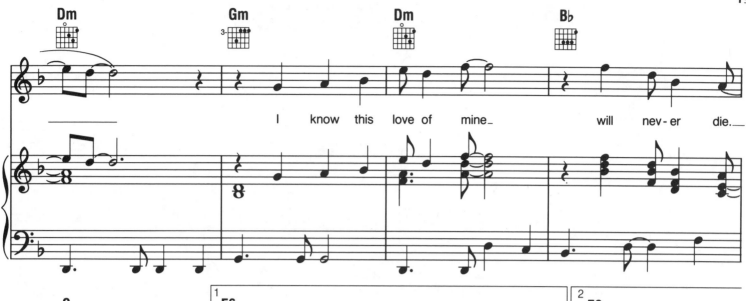

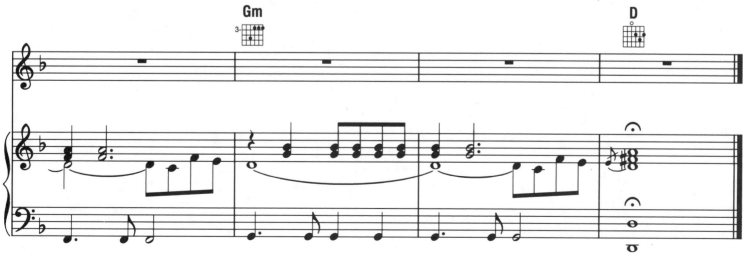

# AND I LOVE YOU SO

Words and Music by
DON McLEAN

MCA music publishing

# ANNIVERSARY SONG

By AL JOLSON
and SAUL CHAPLIN

Dear, as I held you so close in my arms,

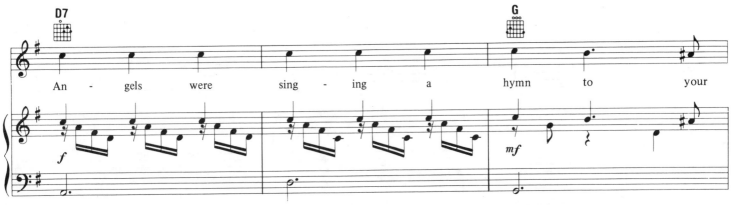

An - gels were sing - ing a hymn to your

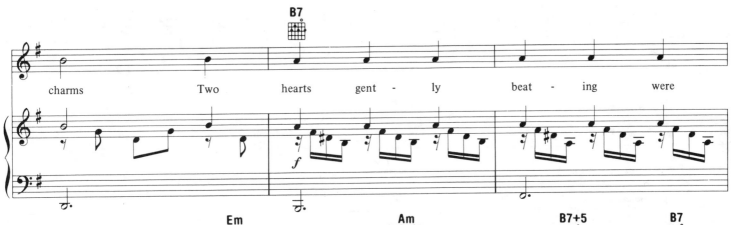

charms Two hearts gent - ly beat - ing were

mur - mur - ing low "My dar - ling, I love you

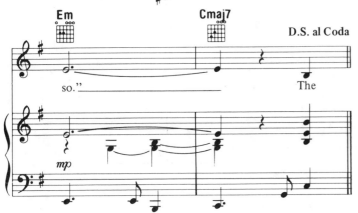

so." _____ The

D.S. al Coda

time. _____

# AND THIS IS MY BELOVED
## (From "KISMET")

Words and Music by ROBERT WRIGHT and GEORGE FORREST
(Music Based on Themes of A. BORODIN)

Lyrics: Dawn's promising skies, Pet-als on a pool drift-ing; Im-ag-ine these in one pair of eyes, And this is my be-

# THE ANNIVERSARY WALTZ

Words and Music by
AL DUBIN and DAVE FRANKLIN

Moderately

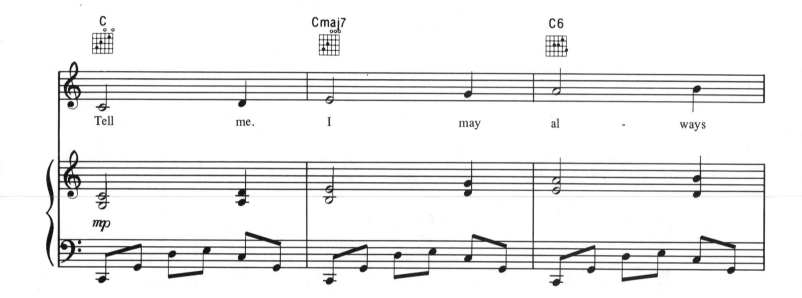

Tell me. I may al - ways

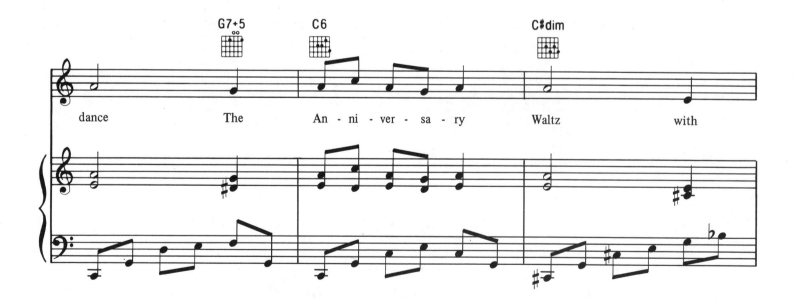

dance The An - ni - ver - sa - ry Waltz with

you._____ Tell me this is

real ro - mance, An an - ni - ver - sa - ry

dream come true._____ Let

this be the an - them to our fu - ture

ped.

32

# CAN'T HELP FALLING IN LOVE

Words and Music by GEORGE DAVID WEISS,
HUGO PERETTI, and LUIGI CREATORE

**Moderately Slow**

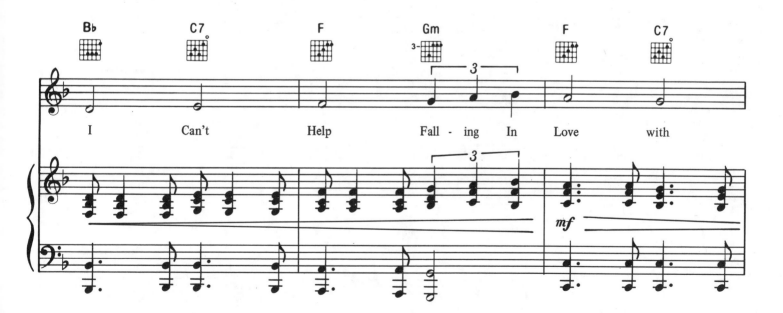

# AVE MARIA
## (The melody adapted to the First Prelude of the Well-tempered Clavier of Johann Sebastian Bach)

CHARLES GOUNOD
English Text from ST. LUKE

44418

Do - - mi-nus te - cum, be - ne -
God_____ is__ with_____ thee. Bless - ed,—

dic - ta tu in mu - li -
bless - ed art thou, art thou_____ a-bove all

e - - ri-bus et_____ be - ne - dic - tus
wo - - men, Bless - ed be thine off - - spring,

fruc - - tus_____ ven - - tris_____
Bless - - ed be thy son,_____ the son of

tu - i Je - - sus._____ Sanc - ta Ma-
God, the Lord most high!_____ Bless - - ed Ma-

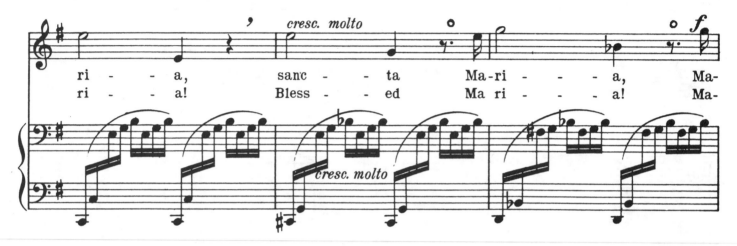

ri - - a, sanc - ta Ma-ri - - a, Ma-
ri - - a! Bless - - ed Ma ri - - a! Ma-

ri - - a, o - - ra pro no - - bis,
ri - - a! Pray,_____ oh, pray__ for_____ us,

no - - - bis pec - ca - to - - ri - bus,
for_____ us wretch - ed sin - - - ners,

nunc_____ et\_\_\_ in ho - - - - ra, in
Now_____ and when the hour_____ of our

ho - - - - ra\_\_\_ mor - tis\_\_\_ nos - trae,
death_____ our\_\_\_ death\_ o'er - takes\_ us,\_\_\_

A - - - - - men!
A - - - - - men!

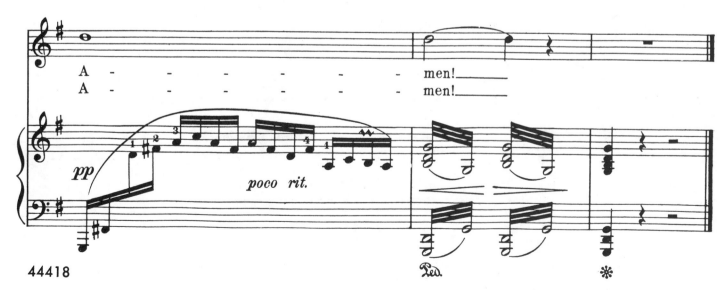

A - - - - - men!_____
A - - - - - men!_____

44418

# AVE MARIA

Very slowly

Music by FRANZ SCHUBERT
Traditional liturgical text

*pronounced grah - tsee - ah

na, A - ve, A - ve! Do - mi - nus Do - mi - nus____ te - cum, Be - ne -

di - cta tu in mu - li - e - ri - bus, et be - ne - di - ctus, et

be - ne - di - ctus fru - ctus ven - tris, ven - tris, tu - i, Je - sus.**

A - ve Ma - ri - a!

** pronounced yeh - zoos

To Coda

A - ve Ma - ri -

a! Ma - ter De - i, O - ra pro no - bis pec - ca -

to - ri - bus, O - ra, o - ra pro no - bis, O - ra, o - ra pro no -

bis, pec - ca - to - ri - bus, nunc et in ho - ra mor - tis, In

ho - ra mor - tis no - strae, in ho - ra mor - tis, mor - tis no - strae, in

ho - ra mor - tis no - strae. A - ve Ma - ri -

D.S. al Coda

a!

CODA

dim.

# BECAUSE

Words by EDWARD TESCHEMACHER
Music by GUY D' HARDELOT

# BECAUSE I LOVE YOU
## (The Postman Song)

Words and Music by
WARREN ALLEN BROOKS

1. I got your let - ter   from the post -
2.,3. If you should feel __   that

man just the oth - er day ___   so I de - cid - ed to write you __ this song
I don't __ real - ly care ___   and that you're start - ing to __ lose ground.

# BRIDAL CHORUS
### (From "Lohengrin")

RICHARD WAGNER

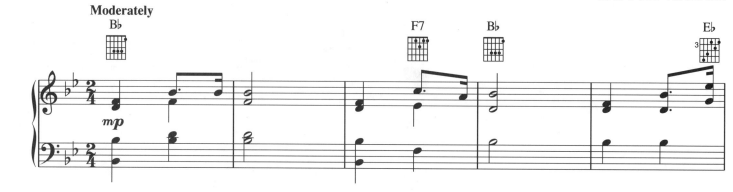

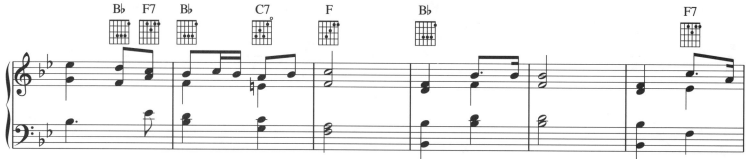

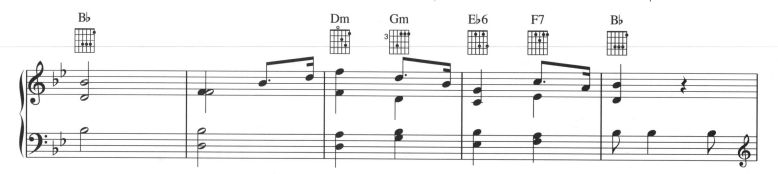

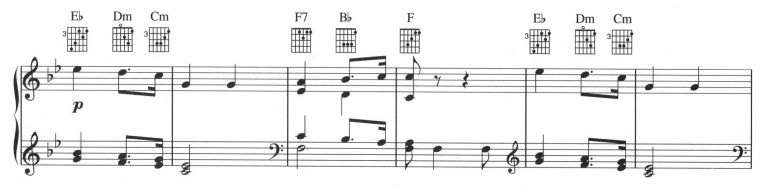

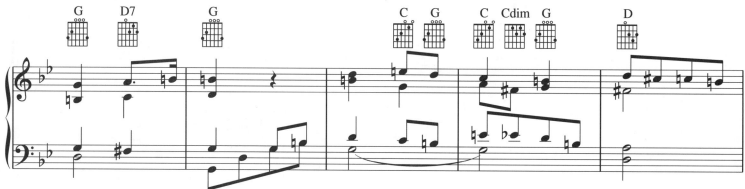

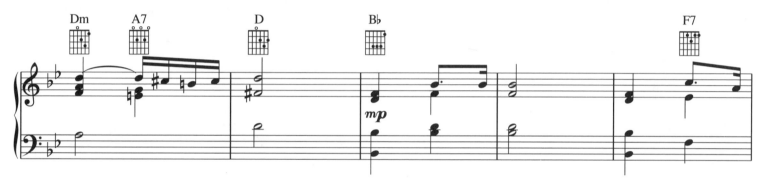

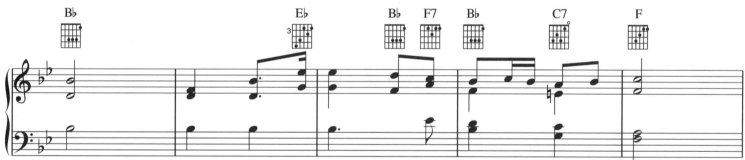

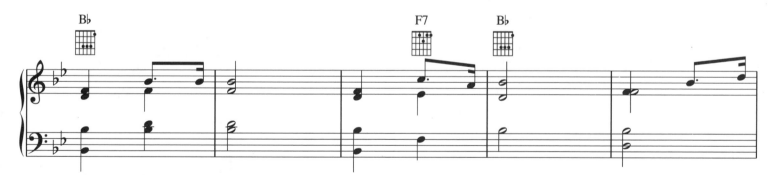

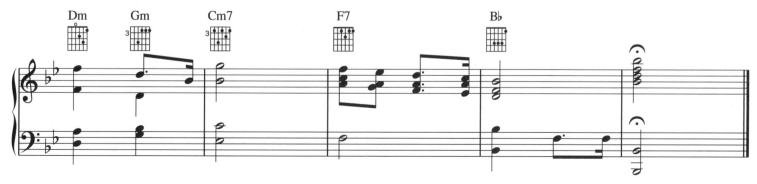

# (THEY LONG TO BE)
# CLOSE TO YOU

Lyric by HAL DAVID
Music by BURT BACHARACH

stars     fall down from the   sky       ev -'ry   time       you walk

by?               Just like   me___      they long   to   be

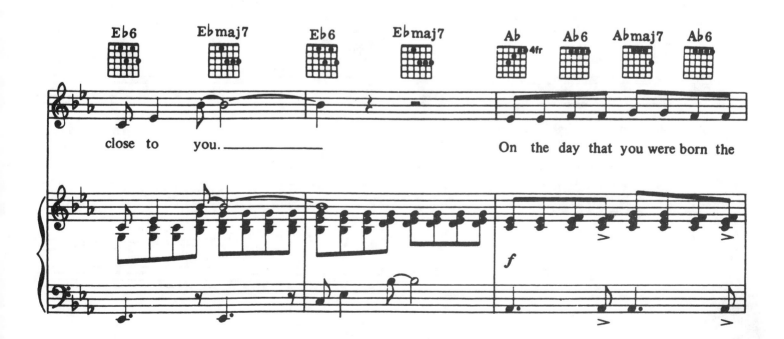

close to    you._____            On   the day that you were born the

# COULD I HAVE THIS DANCE

Words and Music by WAYLAND HOLYFIELD
and BOB HOUSE

Moderately Slow

I'll al- ways re- mem- ber the song they were play- ing, the
al- ways re- mem- ber that mag- ic mo- ment, when

first time _____ we danced and I knew.
I held _____ you close to me.
As we
As

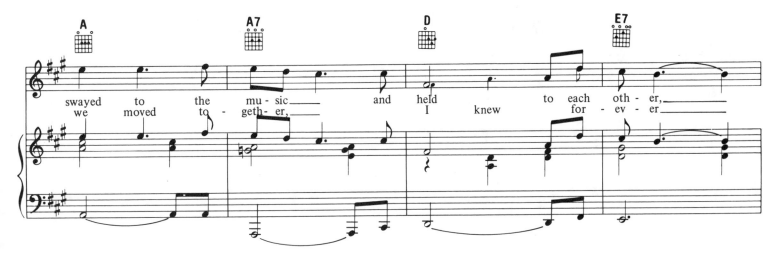

swayed to the mu - sic,\_\_\_\_ and held to each oth - er,\_\_\_\_\_

we to moved to - geth - er,\_\_\_\_ I knew for - ev - er\_\_\_\_\_

I fell in love with\_\_\_\_ you.

you're all I'll ev - er\_\_\_\_ need.

Could

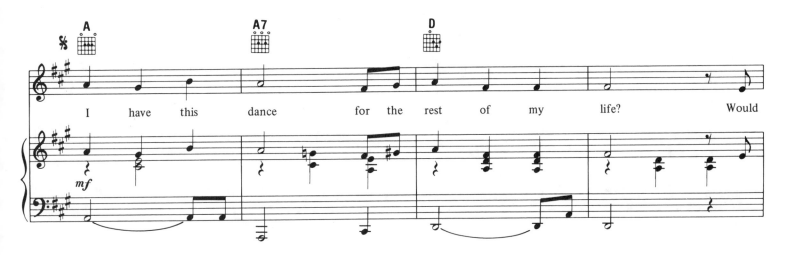

I have this dance for the rest of my life? Would

you be my part - ner\_\_\_\_\_ ev - 'ry night?

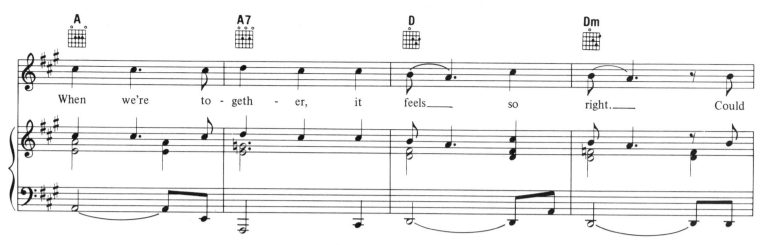

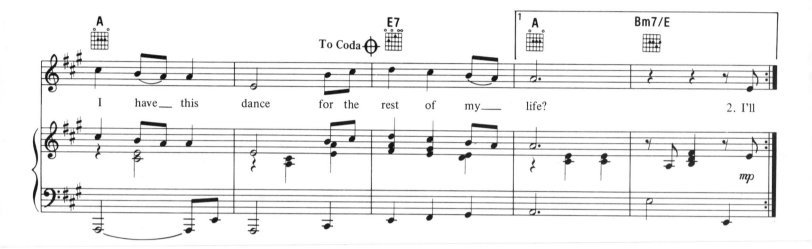

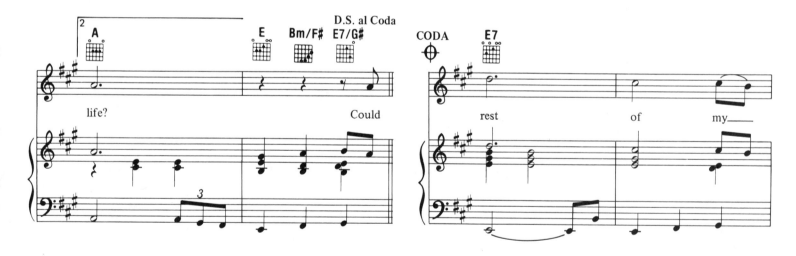

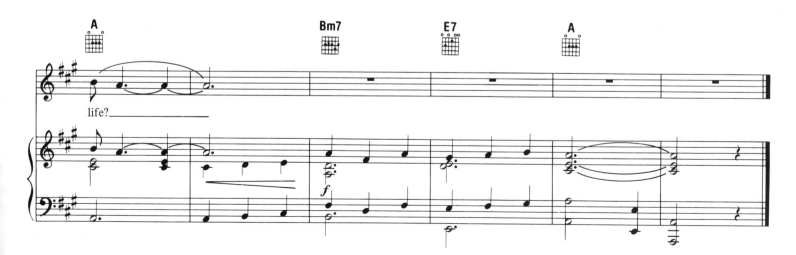

# DEDICATED TO THE ONE I LOVE

Words and Music by LOWMAN PAULING
and RALPH BASS

I'm far a-way from you my ba-by, I

know it's hard for you my ba-by, Be-

# DEVOTED TO YOU

Words and Music by BOUDLEAUX BRYANT

Darling, you can count__ on me

till the sun dries up__ the sea Un - til then I'll al - ways be de -

vot - ed to you. I'll be yours thru end - less time, I'll a - dore your

charms__ sub - lime Guess by now you know that I'm de - vot - ed

# DON'T KNOW MUCH

Words and Music by BARRY MANN,
CYNTHIA WEIL and TOM SNOW

Look at this face, I know the years are show-ing.

Look at this life, I still don't know where it's go-ing.

I don't know much, but I know I love you, and

MCA music publishing

# DREAMS TO DREAM
## (Finale Version)
### (From the Universal Motion Picture "AN AMERICAN TAIL: FIEVEL GOES WEST")

Words and Music by
JAMES HORNER and WILL JENNINGS

# ENDLESS LOVE

Words and Music by
LIONEL RICHIE

**Moderately Slow**

My love, — there's on-ly you in my life, —
Two hearts, — two hearts that you beat as one;

the on-ly thing that's right. — My first love, —
our lives have just be-gun. For-ev-er, —

you're ev-'ry breath that I take, — you're ev-'ry
I'll hold you close in my arms, — I can't re-

# EASY TO LOVE
## (From "BORN TO DANCE")

Words and Music by
COLE PORTER

# FEELINGS

## (¿Dime?)

English Words and Music by MORRIS ALBERT
Spanish Lyric by THOMAS FUNDORA

**Moderately Slow**

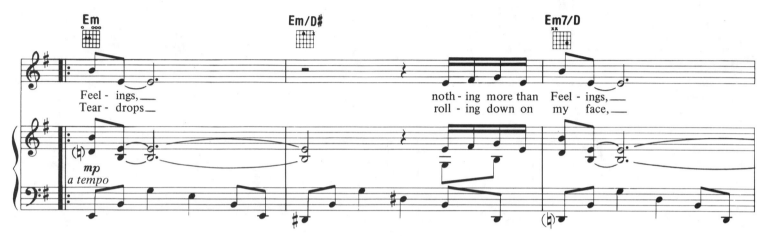

Feel - ings,___ noth - ing more than Feel - ings,___
Tear - drops___ roll - ing down on my face,___

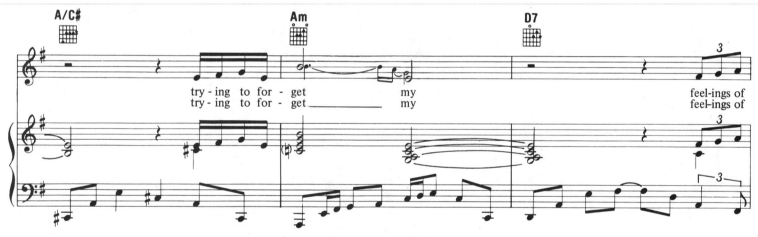

try - ing to for - get my feel-ings of
try - ing to for - get my feel-ings of

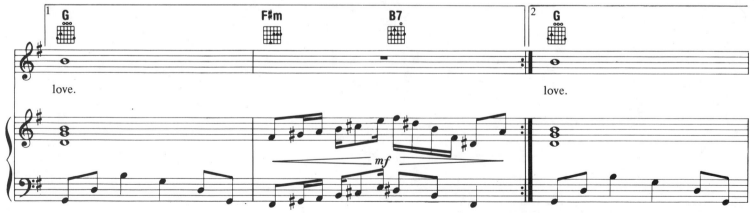

love.  love.

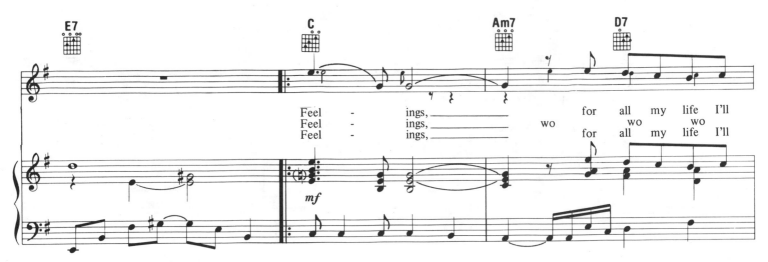

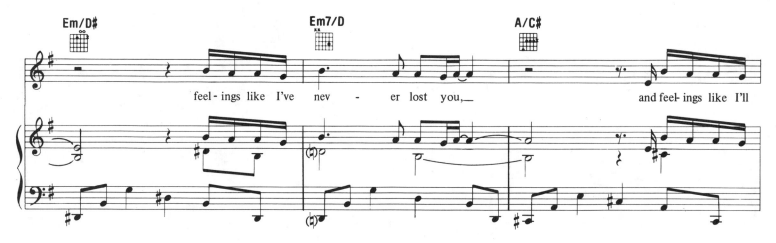

feel - ings like I've nev - er lost you,__ and feel - ings like I'll

nev - er have you__ a - gain in my {heart. life.}

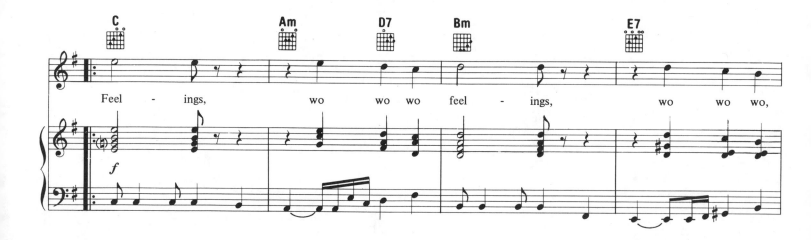

Feel - ings, wo wo wo feel - ings, wo wo wo,

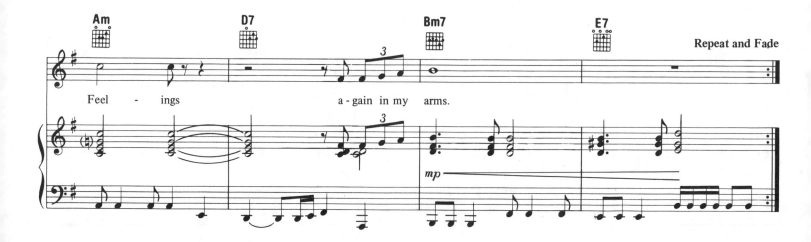

Repeat and Fade

Feel - ings a - gain in my arms.

# FOR ALL WE KNOW

(From the Motion Picture "LOVERS AND OTHER STRANGERS")

Words by ROBB WILSON and JAMES GRIFFIN
Music by FRED KARLIN

Moderato, with a light beat

### (I Love You)
# FOR SENTIMENTAL REASONS

Words by DEEK WATSON
Music by WILLIAM BEST

Slowly

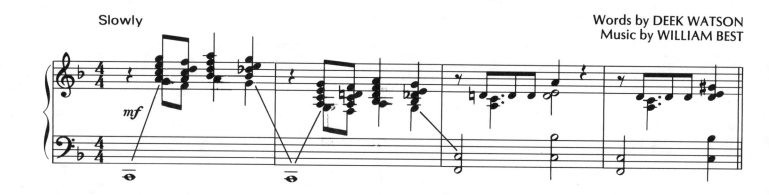

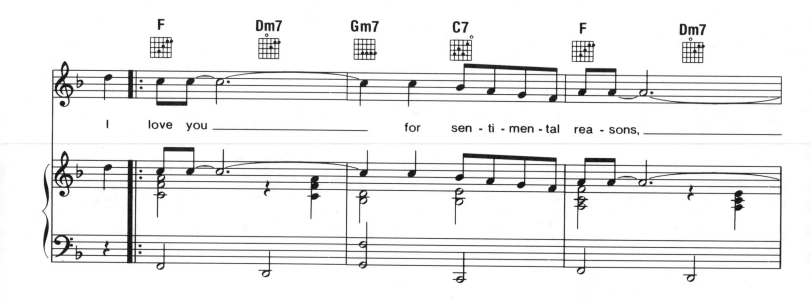

I love you _____ for sen - ti - men - tal rea - sons, _____

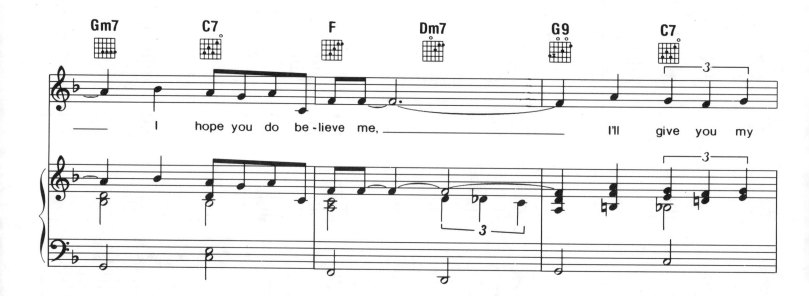

_____ I hope you do be - lieve me, _____ I'll give you my

# FOREVER AND EVER, AMEN

Words and Music by DON SCHLITZ
and PAUL OVERSTREET

Oh ba - by,
Oh dar - lin'   I'm gon - na love____ you for ev -

- er,____ for - ev - er and ev -

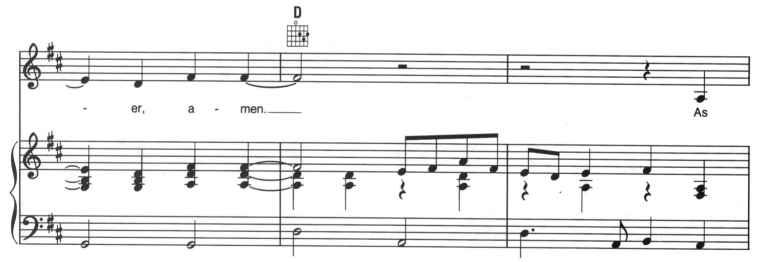

- er, a - men.____ As

long as old men____ sit and talk a - bout__ the wea -

I'm gon-na love____ you for-ev-er and ev-er, for-

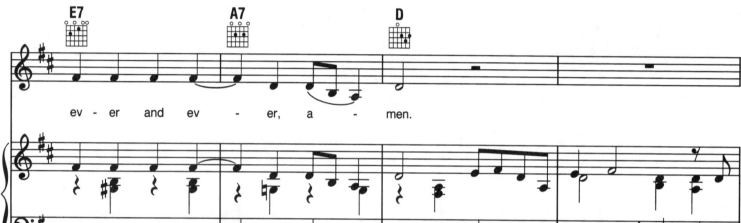

ev-er and ev-er, a-men.

They say

# THE GIRL THAT I MARRY

Words and Music by
IRVING BERLIN

# GROW OLD WITH ME

Words and Music by
JOHN LENNON

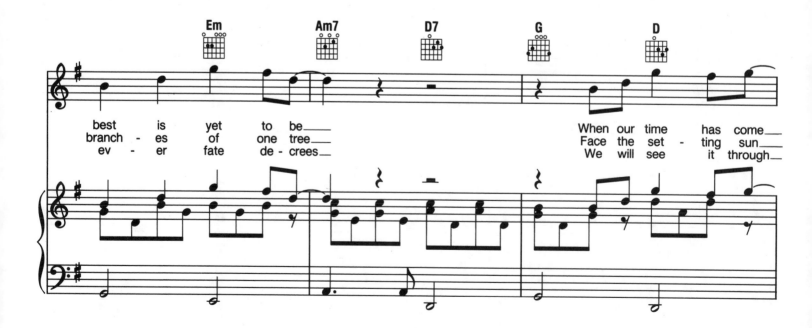

# THE HAWAIIAN WEDDING SONG

English Words by AL HOFFMAN and DICK MANNING
Hawaiian Words and Music by CHARLES E. KING

Slowly, with much warmth

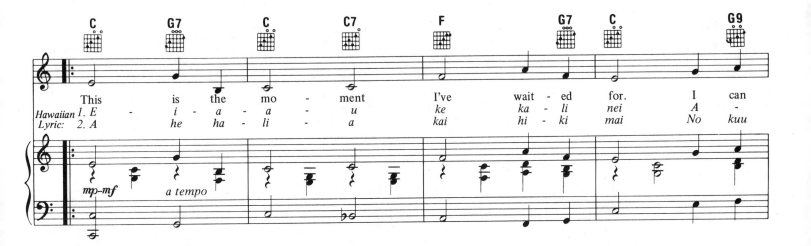

This is the mo - ment I've wait - ed for. I can

*Hawaiian* 1. E i - a - a - u ke ka - li nei A
*Lyric:* 2. A he ha - li - a kai hi - ki mai No kuu

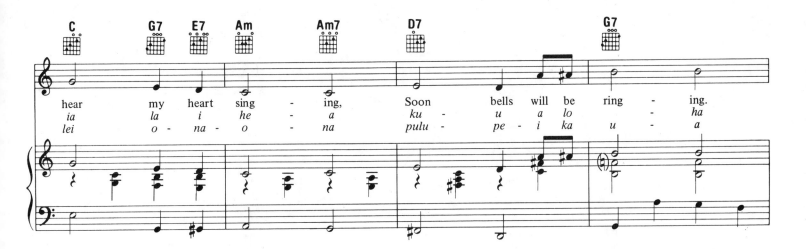

hear my heart sing - ing, Soon bells will be ring - ing.

ia la i he - a ku - u a lo - ha
lei o - na - o - na pulu - pe - i ka u a

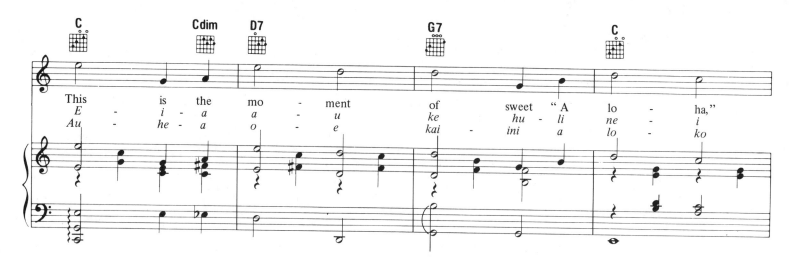

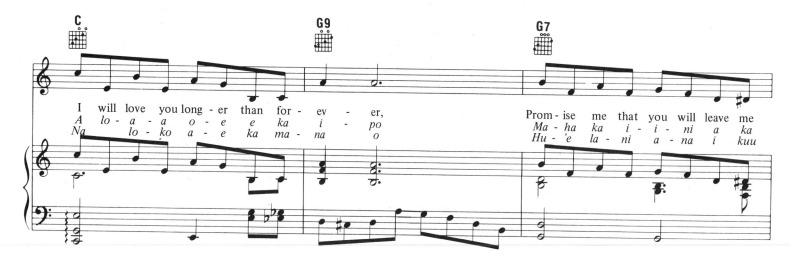

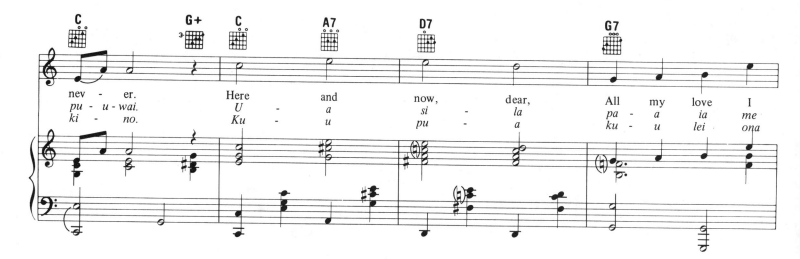

I will love you long - er than for - ev - er.___ Now that we are
Ka - 'u ia e le - i a - e ne - i la
Me ke a - la pu - a pi - ka - ke Nou no we ka i -
A o oe kuu

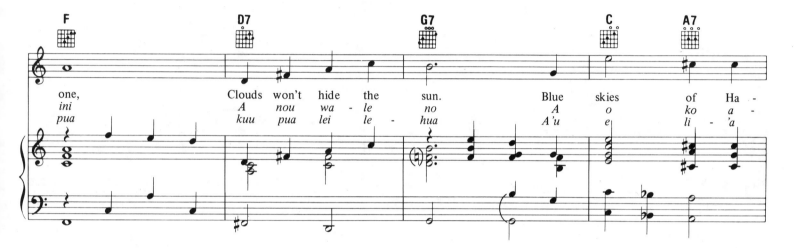

one, Clouds won't hide the sun. Blue skies of Ha -
ini pua A nou wa - le no A o ko a -
pua kuu pua lei le - hua A'u e li - 'a

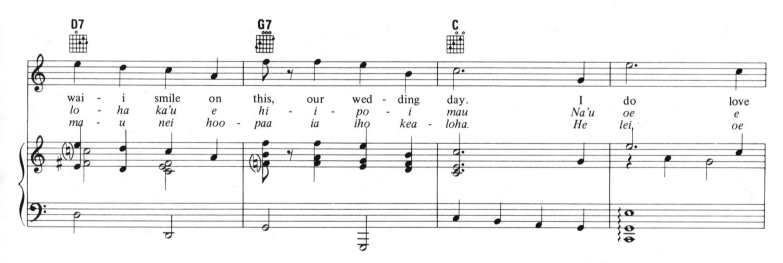

wai - i smile on this, our wed - ding day. I do love
lo - ha ka'u e hi - i - po - i mau Na'u oe e
ma - u nei hoo - paa ia iho kea - loha. He lei, oe

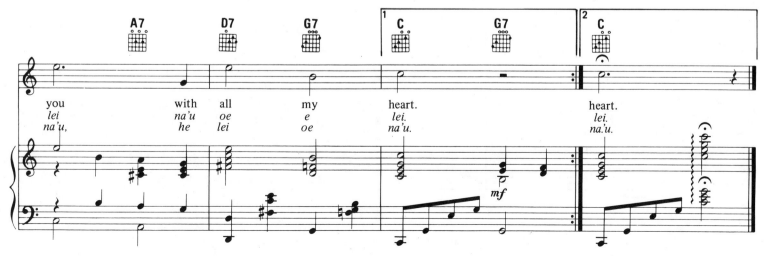

you with all my heart. heart.
lei na'u oe e lei. lei.
na'u, he lei oe na'u. na'u.

# HERE AND NOW

Words and Music by TERRY STEELE
and DAVID ELLIOT

F#m7(♭5)  B7(♭9)  Cmaj7  G/B

share makes life so sweet. To-
more and more each day.

C(add9)/E  Cm6/E♭  G/D  C(add9)

geth-er we'll al - ways be.
Noth - ing can take your love a - way.

G(add9)/B  B7/D#  Em7  G/B

This pledge of love feels so right, and ooh, I need
More than ah - just a dream. I need

Cmaj9  F#m7(♭5)  A/B

you.
you. Yeah. Here and now,

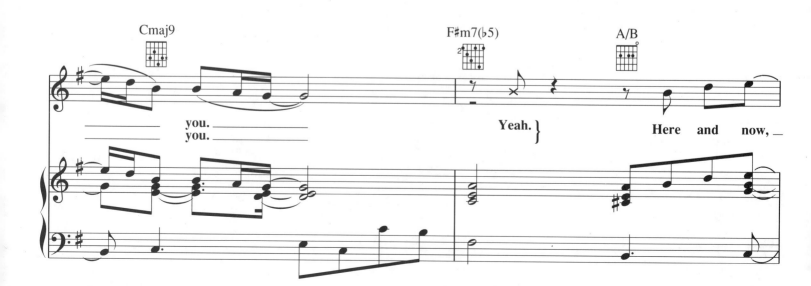

glad to take __ the vow. Here and __ now, _____ oh, ____ I

D.S. al Coda

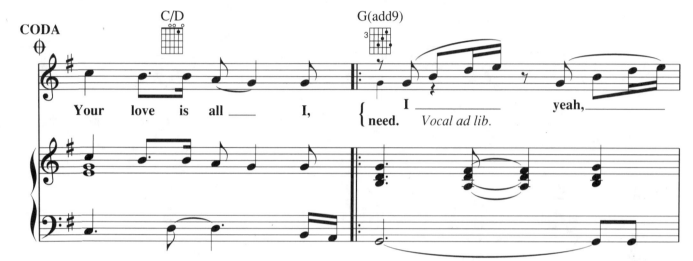

CODA

Your love is all ___ I, { need. *Vocal ad lib.* I _____ yeah, _____

yeah. _____ Uh, yeah. _____ Ay ah, ___ love is all __ I

*last time rit.*

Yeah. _____

# HOW DEEP IS YOUR LOVE

Words and Music by BARRY GIBB,
MAURICE GIBB and ROBIN GIBB

feel you in my arms a - gain. ___
sav - ior when I fall. ___ And you come ___ to me ___ on a sum -
And you may ___ not think ___ I ___ care

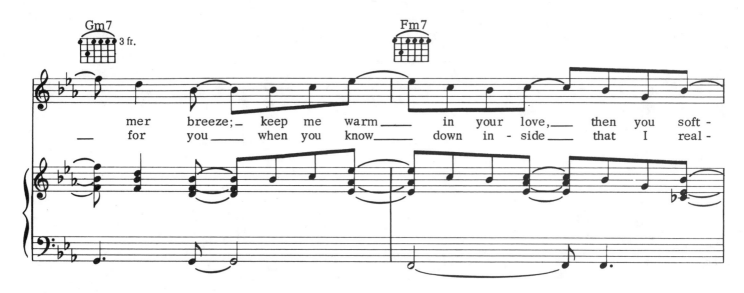

mer breeze; ___ keep me warm ___ in your love, ___ then you soft -
for you ___ when you know ___ down in - side ___ that I real -

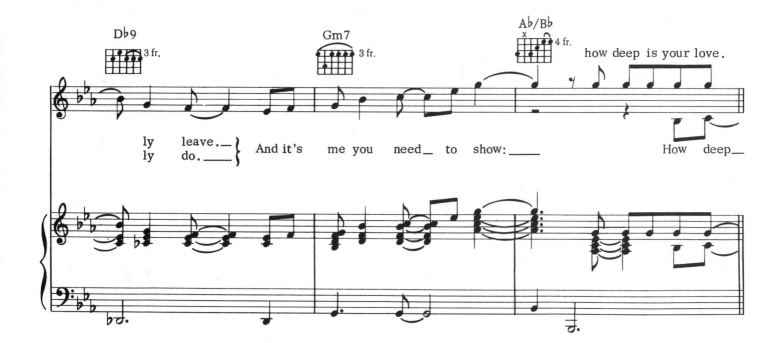

ly leave. ___ } And it's me you need ___ to show: ___ how deep is your love.
ly do. ___ }
How deep ___

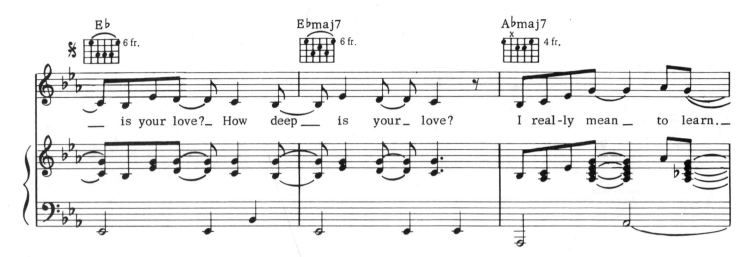

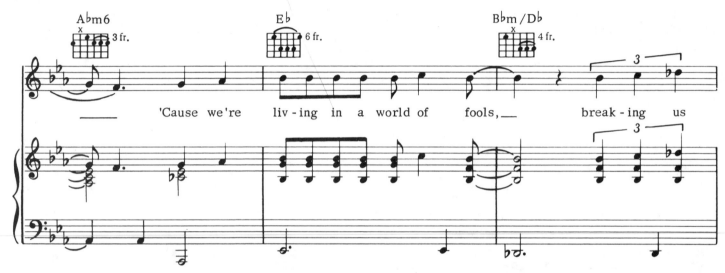

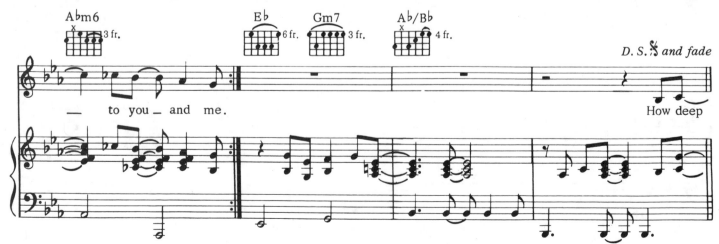

# I CHOSE RIGHT

(From The Musical "BABY")

Lyrics by RICHARD MALTBY, JR.
Music by DAVID SHIRE

then I look at you___ and I know I___ chose

right. Life's a ver-y long road

and the cross-roads come up right a-way.___

And it's sure hard to know which way___ to go___

# I LOVE YOU TRULY

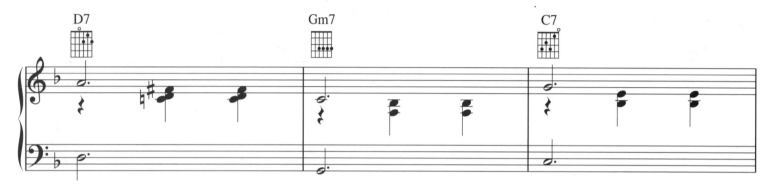

# I PLEDGE MY LOVE

Words by DINO FEKARIS
Music by DINO FEKARIS and FREDDIE PERREN

Ooh, ooh, ooh, ooh, wee, ooh, al- ways to- geth- er, to- geth- er for- ev- er,

al- ways to- geth- er for- ev- er. I will love you 'til the day I die. I know this now and my love won't run dry.

You came a- long, my life has be- gun; Two hearts are now beat- ing as though they were one.

# I'LL BE BY YOUR SIDE

Words and Music by STEVIE B.
and DADGEL ATABAY

look in-side___ your-self___ you will ___ dis-cov ____ er, _____ you'll learn t'ap
look back on ___ the way ___ we grew ___ as lov ____ ers, _____ your

feel that no-one cares _ for you. _ Let all my love _ come shin - ing through _ 'cause

I'll be there _____ for ____ you. _____

When I  I'll be there. _____  When you

feel that no - one cares _ for you, _ and you need some-one _ to  pull __ you through, _ when you

# I'LL ALWAYS LOVE YOU

Words and Music by
JIMMY GEORGE

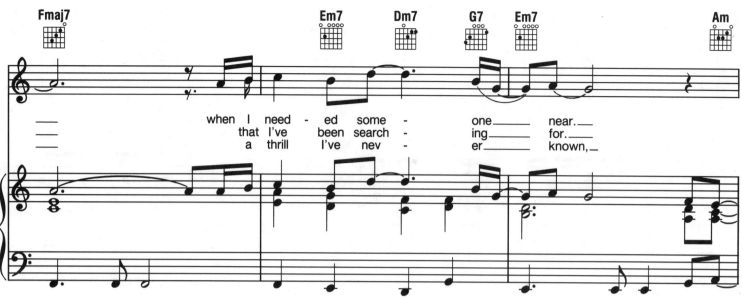

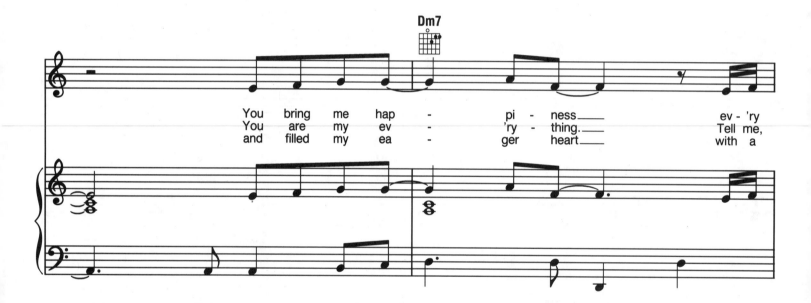

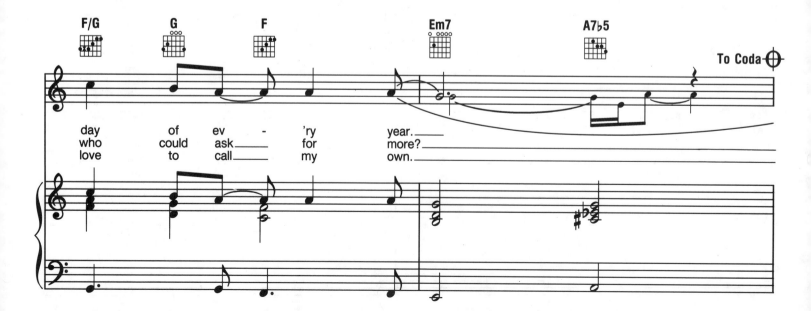

# JESU, JOY OF MAN'S DESIRING

By J.S. BACH

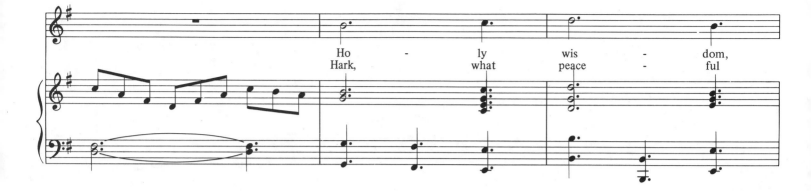

Ho - ly wis - dom,
Hark, what peace - ful

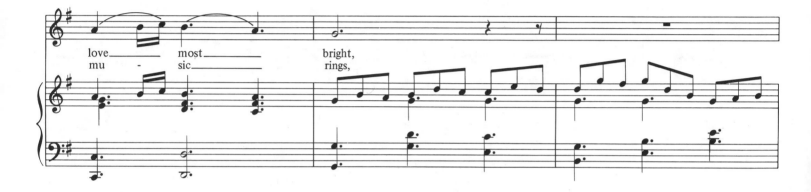

love_____ most_____ bright,
mu - sic_____ rings,

Drawn by the
Where

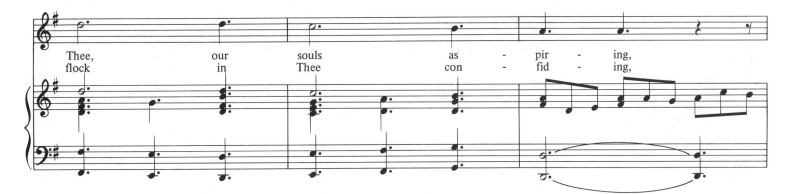

Thee,        our     souls              as  -  pir  -  ing,
flock   in     Thee    con  -  fid  -  ing,

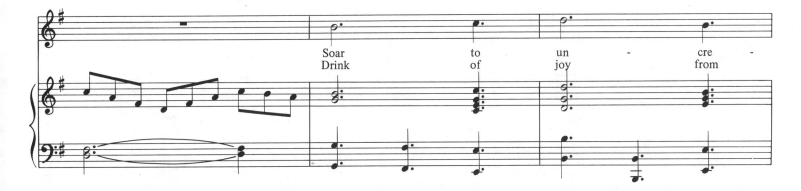

Soar      to      un  -        cre  -
Drink     of      joy        from

at  -  ed _____            light.
death  -  less _____     springs.

Word of God our flesh_____ that
Theirs is beau - ty's fair - est

fash - ioned,
plea - sure,

With the fire of life_____ im -
Theirs is wis - dom's ho - liest

pas - sioned.
trea - sure.

Striv - ing still to truth un -
Thou dost ev - er lead Thine

known,
own,

Soar - ing
In - ing the

dy - ing
love of

round___ Thy___
joys___ un -

throne.
known.

# JUST THE WAY YOU ARE

Words and Music by
BILLY JOEL

# LONGER

Words and Music by
DAN FOGELBERG

Moderate Ballad

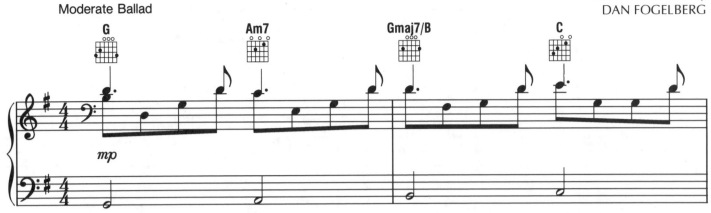

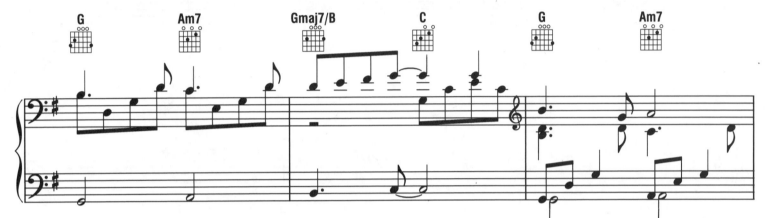

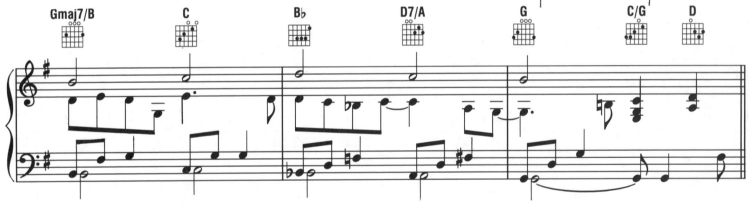

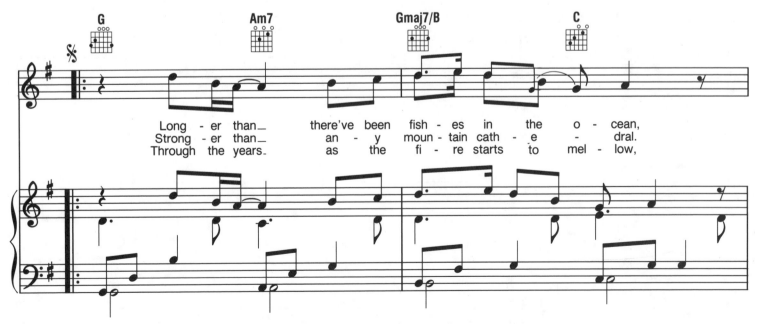

Long - er than____ there've been fish - es in the o - cean,
Strong - er than____ an - y moun - tain cath - e - dral.
Through the years____ as the fi - re starts to mel - low,

high - er than___ an - y bird ev - er flew,___
tru - er than___ an - y tree ev - er grew,___
burn - ing lines___ in the book of our lives.___

Though the

Long - er than___ there've been stars up in the hea - vens,___
Deep - er than___ an - y for - est prim - e - val,___
bind - ing cracks___ and the pag - es start to yel - low,___

I've been in love___ with you.___
I am in love___ with you.___
I'll be in love___ with you.

I'll be in love\_\_\_ with you.\_\_\_

Long - er than\_\_\_ there've been fish - es\_\_\_ in the o - cean,\_\_\_

# THE LAST TIME I FELT LIKE THIS

## (From "SAME TIME, NEXT YEAR")

Words by ALAN BERGMAN
and MARILYN BERGMAN
Music by MARVIN HAMLISCH

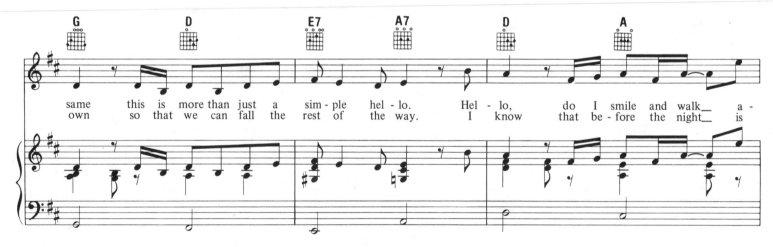

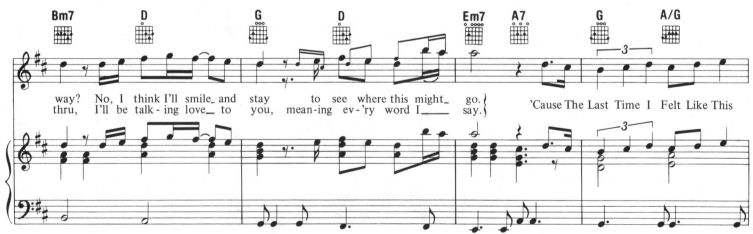

# LOST IN YOUR EYES

Words and Music by
DEBORAH GIBSON

# LOVE IS HERE TO STAY

## (From "GOLDWYN FOLLIES")

Words by IRA GERSHWIN
Music by GEORGE GERSHWIN

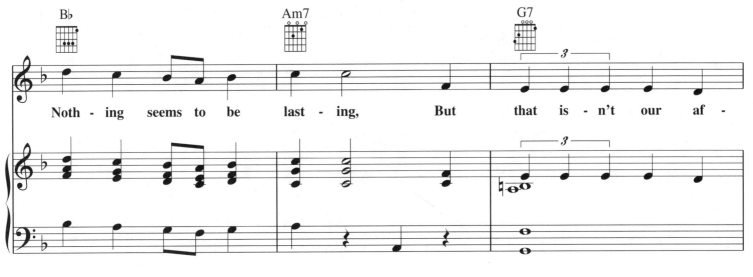

Noth - ing seems to be last - ing, But that is - n't our af -

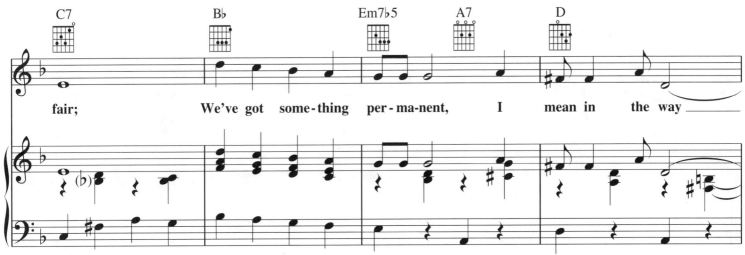

fair; We've got some-thing per - ma-nent, I mean in the way

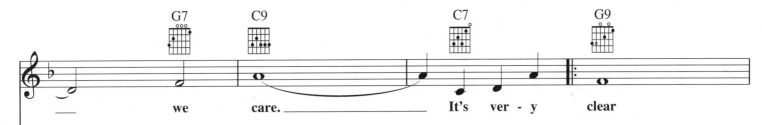

we care. It's ver - y clear

Our love is here to stay; Not for a year

# LOVE ME TENDER

Words and Music by ELVIS PRESLEY,
and VERA MATSON

Moderately slow

Verse

1. Love Me Ten - der, love me sweet;
2. Love Me Ten - der, love me long;
3. Love Me Ten - der, love me dear;

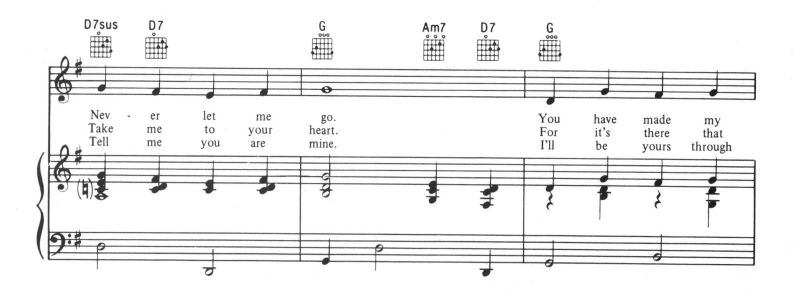

Nev - er let me go.
Take me to your heart.
Tell me you are mine.

You have made my
For it's made there that
I'll be yours through

EXTRA VERSE    4. When at last my dreams come true,
Darling, this I know:
Happiness will follow you
Everywhere you go.

# LOVE OF A LIFETIME

By BILL LEVERTY and CARL SNARE

**Slow Rock Ballad**

I guess the time_ was right_ for us_ to say
make a wish and send it on _ a prayer.

we'd take our time___ and live our lives _ to-geth-
We know our dreams_ can all _ come true _ with

-er day \_ by \_ day. _____
love \_ that we \_\_\_ can _____ share. \_\_\_ \_\_\_

We'll
With

you I nev - er won - der,
"Will you be\_\_ there for \_\_ me?" \_\_\_

With

you I nev - er won - der. \_\_
You're the right \_\_\_\_\_ one \_\_ for _____

\_\_\_ me. \_\_\_
I fi - n'lly found \_ the love \_\_\_\_\_ of a life-

(Fi - n'lly found_ the love _____ of a life - time,) oo, for -

ev - er in ___ my heart. _____ I fi - n'lly found_ the love _____ of a life -

- time. _____ Oo. _____

# LOVING YOU

Words and Music by
MIKE STOLLER and JERRY LEIBER

# LOVE WITHOUT END, AMEN

Words and Music by
AARON G. BARKER

just be - tween___ us."

He said,
I said,

"Dad-dy's don't___ just love___ their chil - dren ev - 'ry now___ and then,___

it's a love with - out end,___ A - men."

It's a love with - out end,___ A - men.

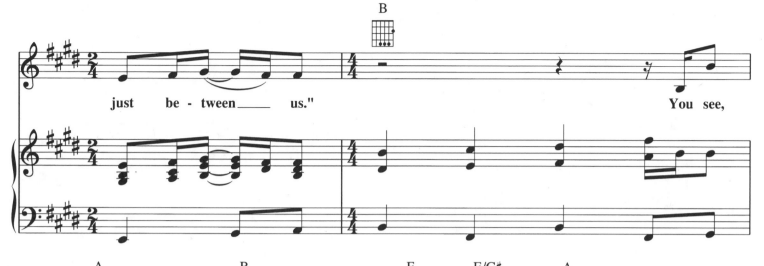

just be - tween___ us." You see,

dad-dy's just_ don't love_ their chil - dren ev - 'ry now_ and then,_____

it's a love with-out end, __ A - men. It's a

love with-out end, __ A - men.

# MAY YOU ALWAYS

Words and Music by LARRY MARKES
and DICK CHARLES

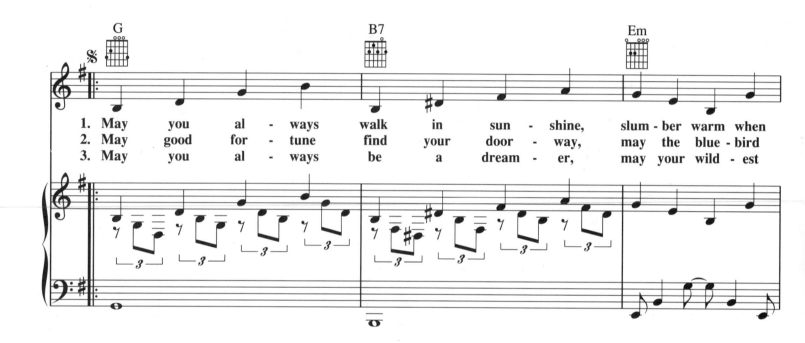

1. May you al - ways walk in sun - shine, slum - ber warm when
2. May good for - tune find your door - way, may the blue - bird
3. May you al - ways be a dream - er, may your wild - est

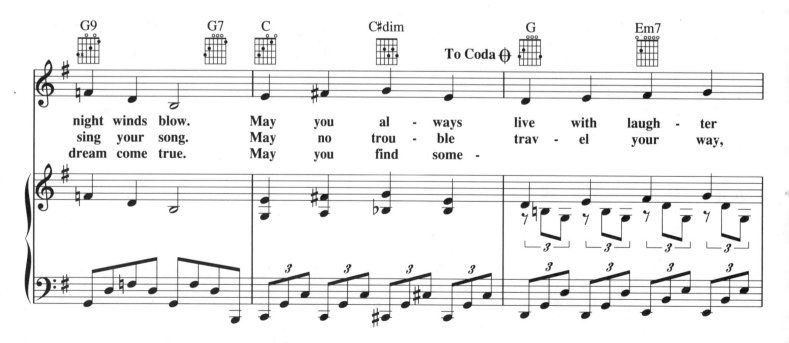

night winds blow. May you al - ways live with laugh - ter
sing your song. May no trou - ble trav - el your way,
dream come true. May you find some -

# MY CUP RUNNETH OVER

## (From "I DO! I DO!")

Words by TOM JONES
Music by HARVEY SCHMIDT

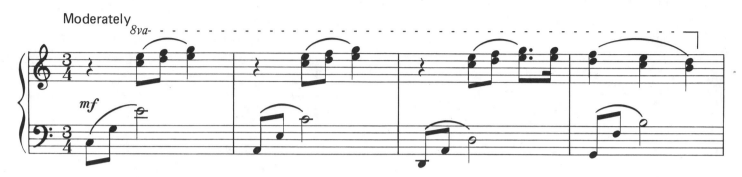

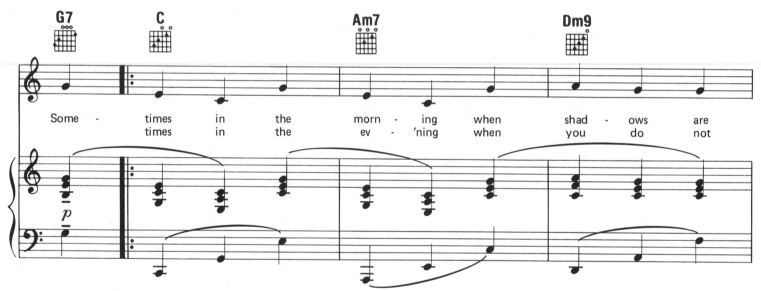

Some - times in the morn - ing when shad - ows are
times in the ev - 'ning when you do not

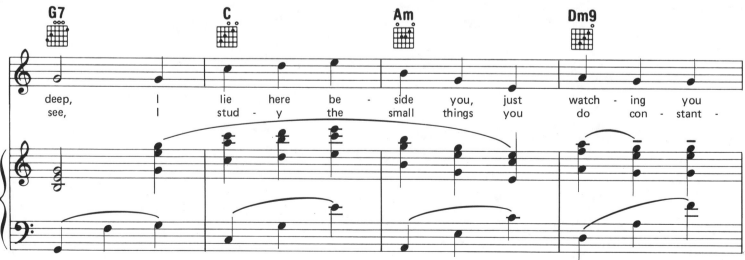

deep, I lie here be - side you, just watch - ing you
see, I stud - y the small things you do con - stant -

# MARRY ME

## (From The Musical "THE RINK")

Lyrics by FRED EBB
Music by JOHN KANDER

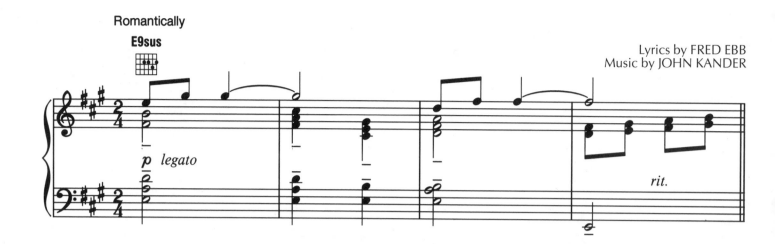

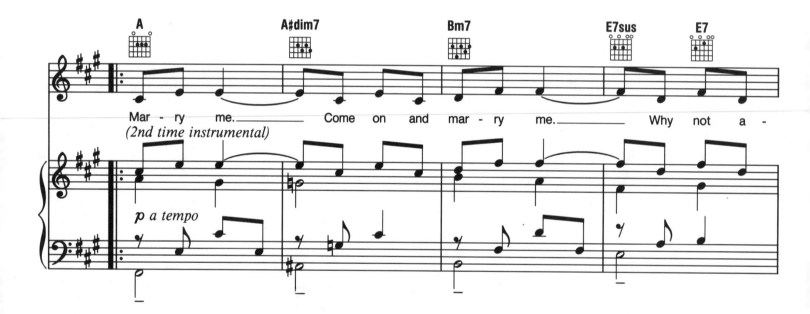

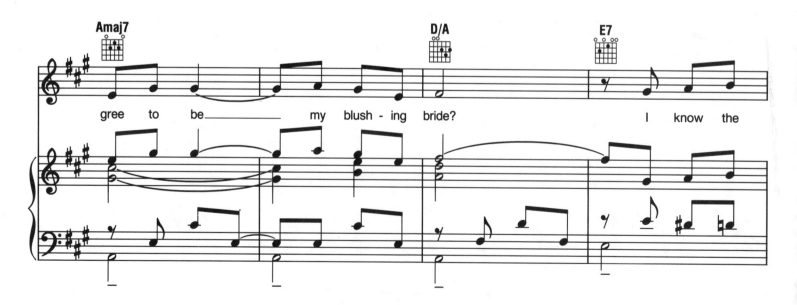

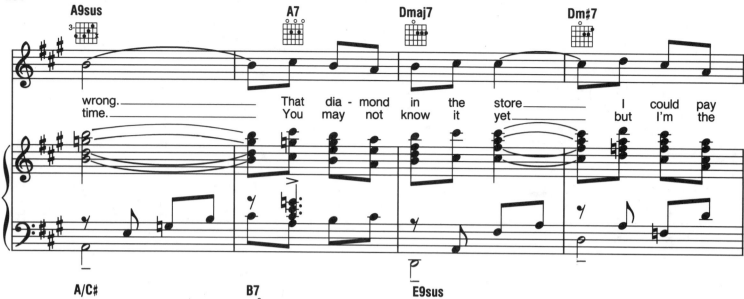

# NEVERTHELESS
## (I'm In Love With You)

Words and Music by
BERT KALMER and HARRY RUBY

# OH, PROMISE ME!

Words by CLEMENT SCOTT
Music by REGINALD de KOVEN

With a flowing movement

Oh

prom-ise me that some-day you and I_____ will take our love to-geth-er to some

sky_____ Where we can be a-lone and faith re-new_____ And

# PEOPLE WILL SAY WE'RE IN LOVE

## (From "OKLAHOMA!")

Lyrics by OSCAR HAMMERSTEIN II
Music by RICHARD RODGERS

# SO AMAZING

Words and Music by
LUTHER VANDROSS

Slowly with feeling

Love has_____ tru-ly_____ been_ good to___ me.
Got to_____ tell_ you_ how_ you thrill___ me.

Not__ e-ven__ one sad__ day, or min-ute have__ I had__ since you've come__ my way.
I'm hap-py as__ I can__ be. You have come__ and it's changed__ my whole world,___

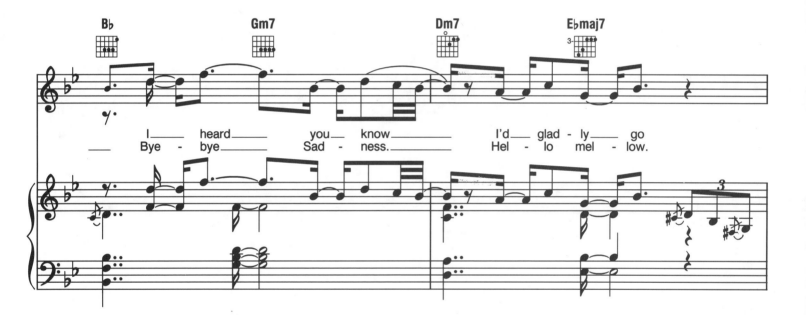

I__ heard_____ you know_____ I'd glad-ly__ go
__ Bye - bye_____ Sad - ness._____ Hel - lo mel - low.

an - y - where__ you take__ me. It's so a-maz-ing to__ be loved.__ I'd
What__ a won - der-ful__ day. It's so a-maz-ing to__ be loved.__ I'd

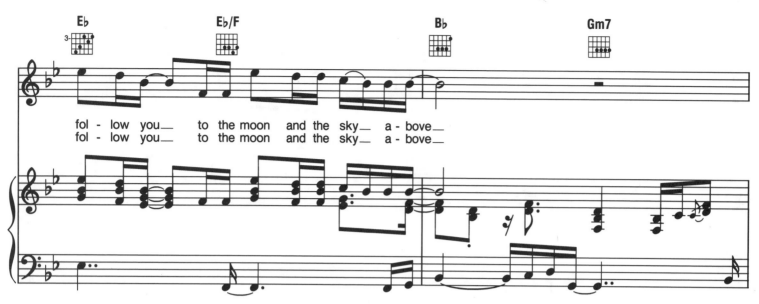

fol - low you___ to the moon___ and the sky___ a - bove___
fol - low you___ to the moon___ and the sky___ a - bove___

oo _____ I'd___ go ___

___ And it's so a -

ma - zing a-ma - zing   I could stay for - e - ver,__ for - e - ver.   Here in love and
ma - zing a-ma - zing   Love for us to - geth - er,__ to - geth - er   I would leave you

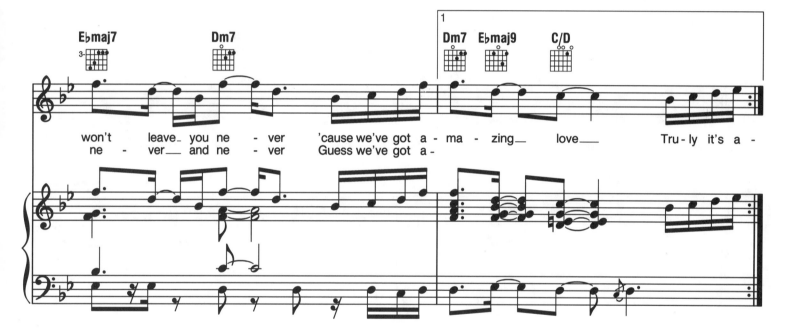

won't   leave__ you ne - ver   'cause we've got a - ma - zing__ love__   Tru - ly it's a-
ne - ver__ and ne - ver   Guess we've got a-

ma - zing__ love__   oo__   So   a - ma - zing

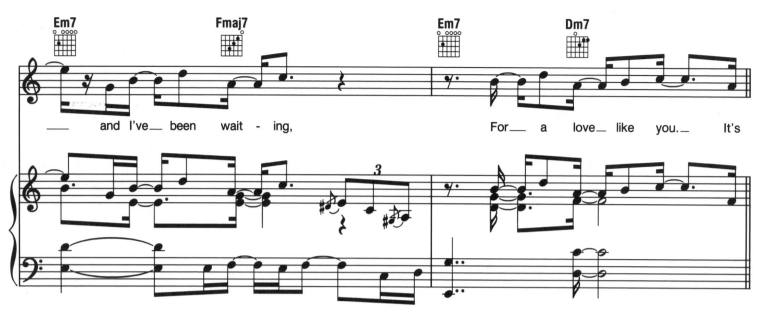

and I've\_ been wait - ing, For\_ a love\_ like you.\_ It's

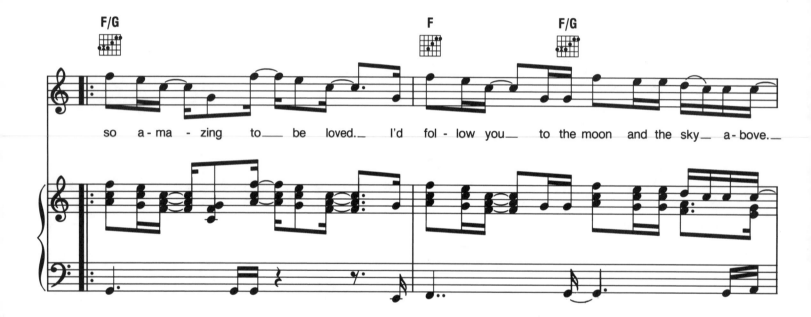

so a - ma - zing to\_ be loved.\_ I'd fol - low you\_ to the moon and the sky\_ a - bove.

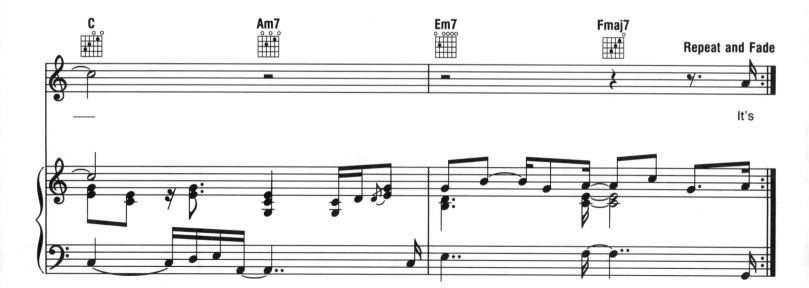

It's

# SOMETHING

Words and Music by
GEORGE HARRISON

Some-thing in___ the way___ she moves,___
Some-where in___ her smile___ she knows,___
Some-thing in___ the way___ she knows,___

at-tracts___ me like___ no oth-er lov-___er.
that I___ don't need___ no oth-er lov-___er.
and all___ I have___ to do is think___ of her.

Some-thing in___ the way___ she woos_____ me.
Some-thing in___ her style___ that shows_____ me.
Some-thing in___ the things___ she shows_____ me.

I don't want to leave___ her now,           you

# SO IN LOVE

## (From "KISS ME KATE")

Words and Music by
COLE PORTER

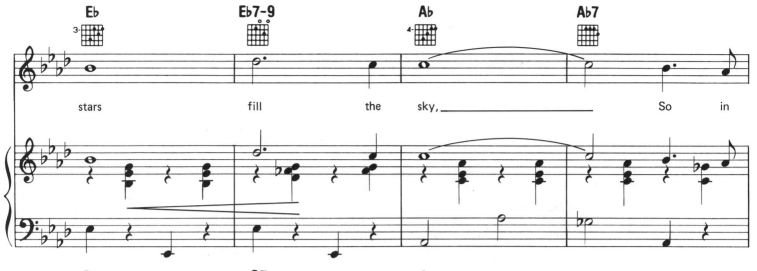

stars fill the sky, _____ So in

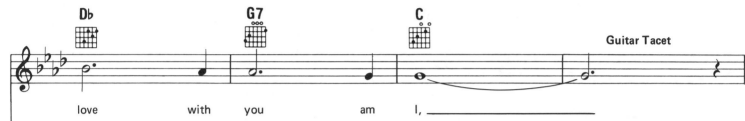

love with you am I, _____

Guitar Tacet

E - ven _____ with - out you, _____ My

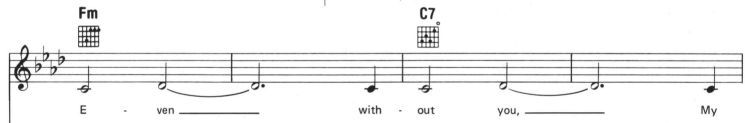

arms fold _____ a - bout you, _____ You

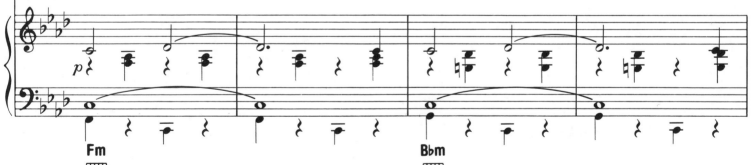

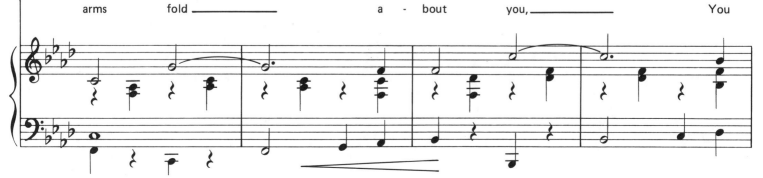

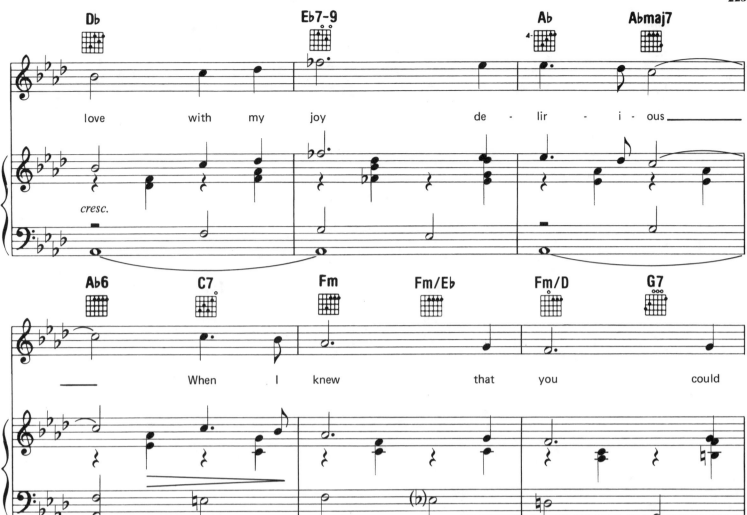

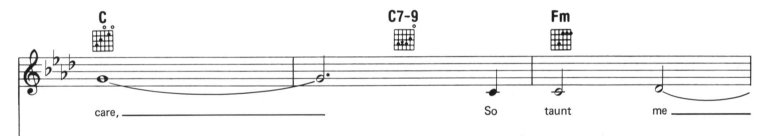

love    with    you,    my    love_____    am

# SOMEWHERE OUT THERE

(From "AN AMERICAN TAIL")

By JAMES HORNER,
BARRY MANN and CYNTHIA WEIL

MCA music publishing

# SUNRISE, SUNSET
## (From "FIDDLER ON THE ROOF")

Words by SHELDON HARNICK
Music by JERRY BOCK

# STRANGER IN PARADISE

## (From "KISMET" and "TIMBUKTU!")

Words and Music by ROBERT WRIGHT and GEORGE FORREST
(Music Based on Themes of A. BORODIN)

# THAT'S WHAT LOVE IS FOR

Words and Music by MARK MUELLER,
MICHAEL OMARTIAN and AMY GRANT

Some-times we make it harder than it is.

We'll take a per-fect night and fill it up with words we don't mean Dark sides best un-seen. And we won-der why we're feel-ing this way.

MCA music publishing

by that's _ what _ love _ is for.___

Guitar solo - ad lib.

Solo ends                                Be -

liev - ing in _ the one_____ thing_ that has got - ten us _ this far.___

244

# THIS I PROMISE YOU

Words and Music by
CLYDE OTIS and VINCENT CORSO

# THROUGH THE YEARS

Words and Music by STEVE DORFF
and MARTY PANZER

**Appreciatively**

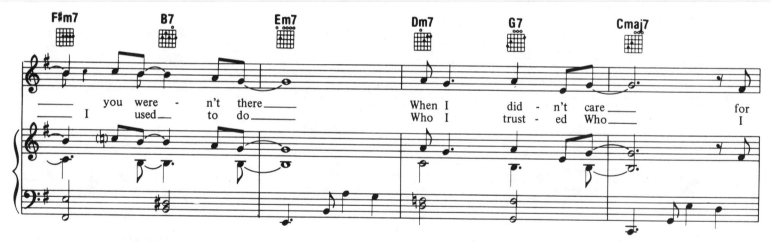

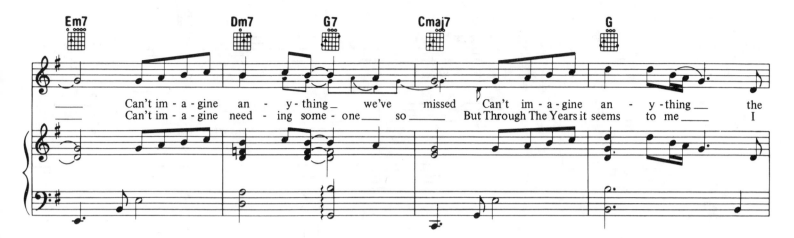

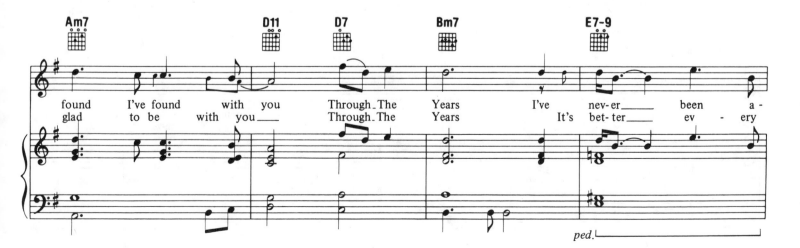

# THE TIES THAT BIND

Words and Music by CLYDE OTIS and VINCENT CORSO

# TILL

Words by CARL SIGMAN
Music by CHARLES DANVERS

Moderately

Till _____ the moon de - serts the sky _____

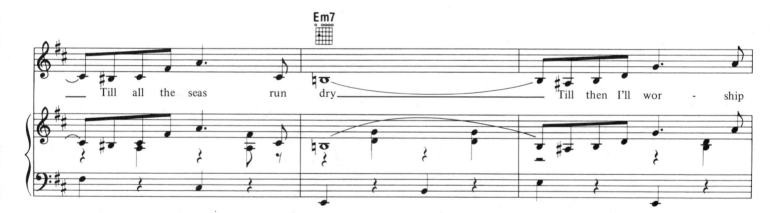

___ Till all the seas run dry _____ Till then I'll wor - ship

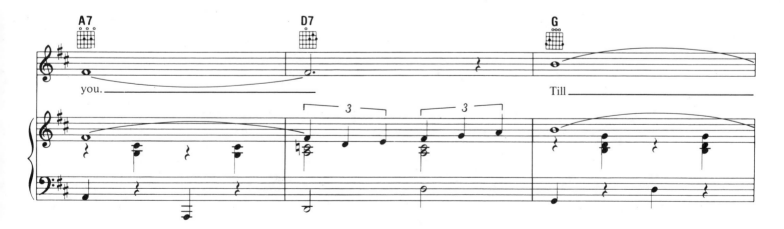

you. _____ Till _____

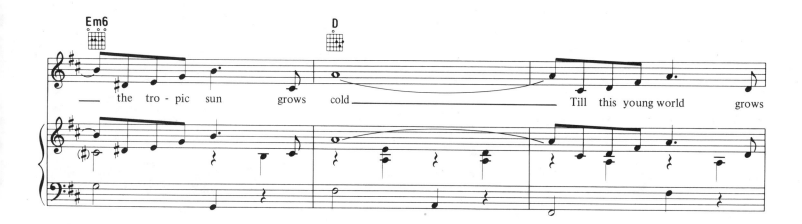

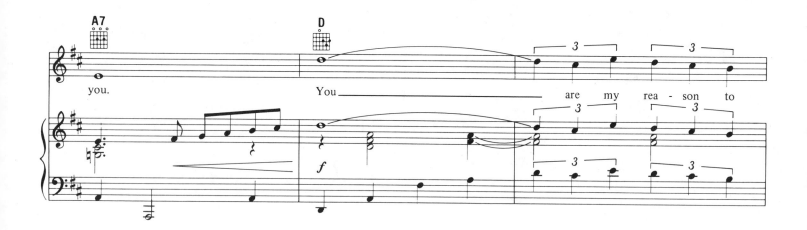

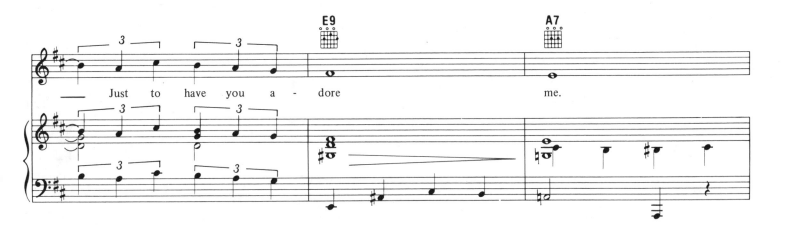

Just to have you a - dore _____ me.

Till _____ the riv - ers flow up - stream _____

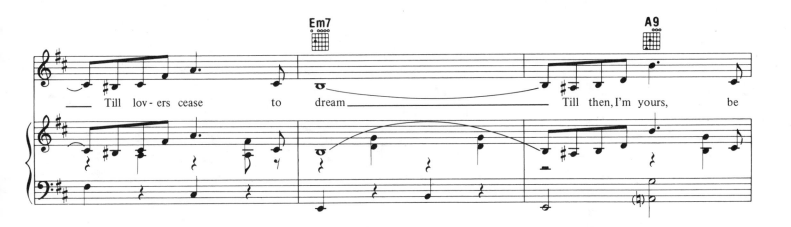

____ Till lov - ers cease to dream _____ Till then, I'm yours, be

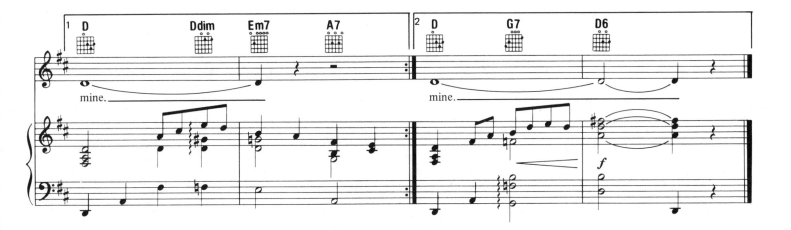

mine. ____ | mine. ____

# TOGETHER

Words and Music by B.G. DESYLVA,
RAY HENDERSON and LEW BROWN

Moderately Slow

8vb

# TRUE LOVE

Words and Music by
COLE PORTER

Moderately Slow

I give to you and you give to me

True Love, True Love. So, on and

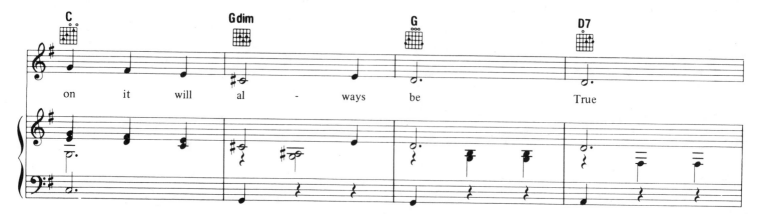

on it will al - ways be True

# TRUMPET TUNE

Stately

JEREMIAH CLARKE

# TRUMPET VOLUNTARY

JEREMIAH CLARKE

Majestically

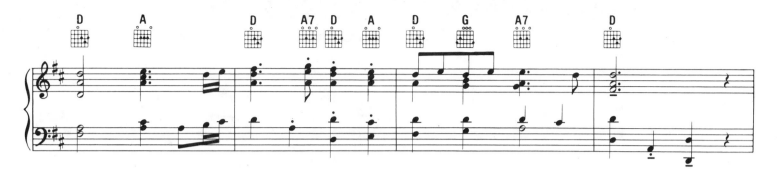

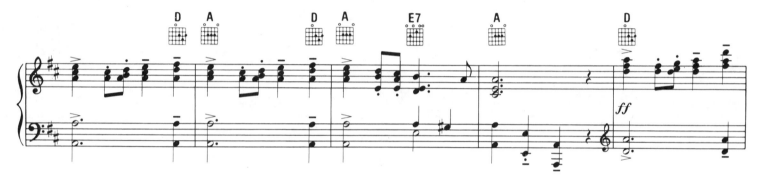

# THE VOWS GO UNBROKEN
## (ALWAYS TRUE TO YOU)

Words and Music by GARY BURR
and ERIC KAZ

MCA music publishing

# TOO MUCH HEAVEN

Words and Music by BARRY GIBB,
MAURICE GIBB, and ROBIN GIBB

Slow Ballad tempo

No - bod - y gets too much heav - en no more, it's much hard - er to come by; I'm

wait - ing in line. _____ No - bod - y gets too much

# WEDDING MARCH

FELIX MENDELSSOHN

Majestically

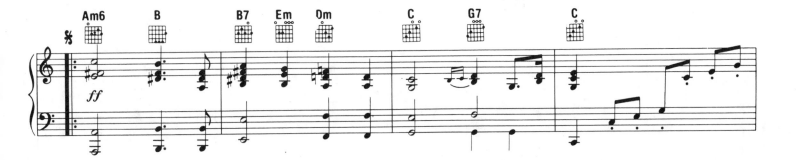

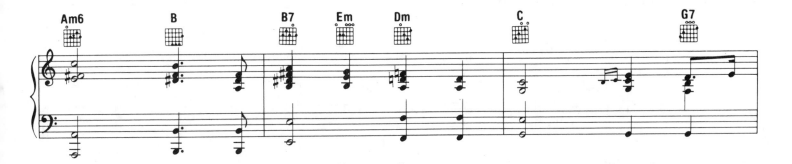

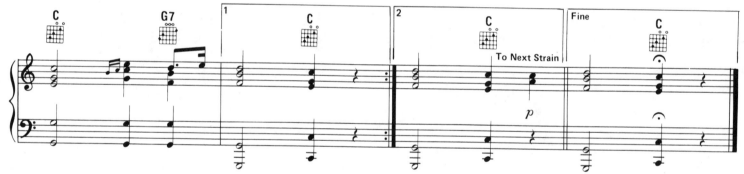

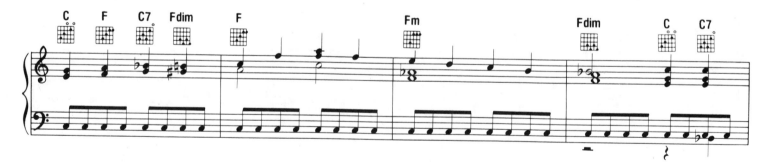

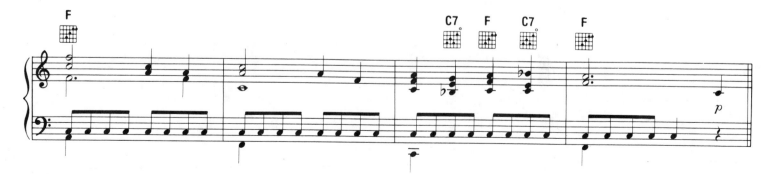

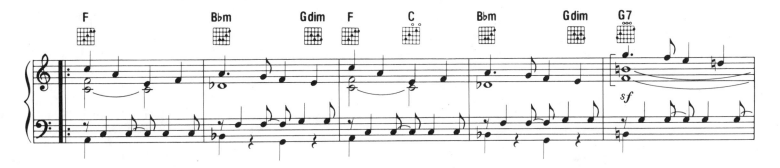

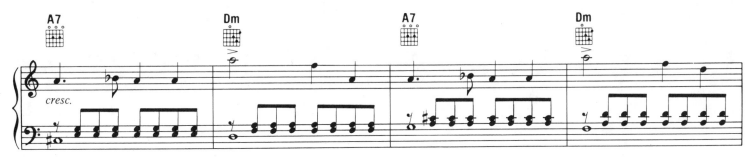

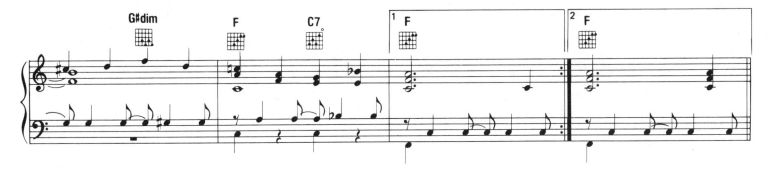

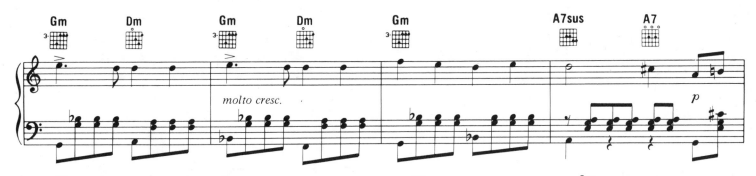

# WEDDING PROCESSIONAL
## (From "THE SOUND OF MUSIC")

Lyrics by OSCAR HAMMERSTEIN II
Music by RICHARD RODGERS

Majestically

**For the entrance of the Bride**

*rit.*     *a tempo*

*ff*     *rit.*

# WHAT THE WORLD NEEDS NOW IS LOVE

Lyric by HAL DAVID
Music by BURT BACHARACH

# WHEN I FALL IN LOVE

Words by EDWARD HEYMAN
Music by VICTOR YOUNG

When I fall in love it will be for-ev-er, or I'll nev-er

fall in love._____ In a rest-less world like this is, love is

end-ed be-fore it's be-gun, and too man-y moon-light kiss-es seem to

# WHEN I'M WITH YOU

Words and Music by
ARNOLD DAVID LANNI

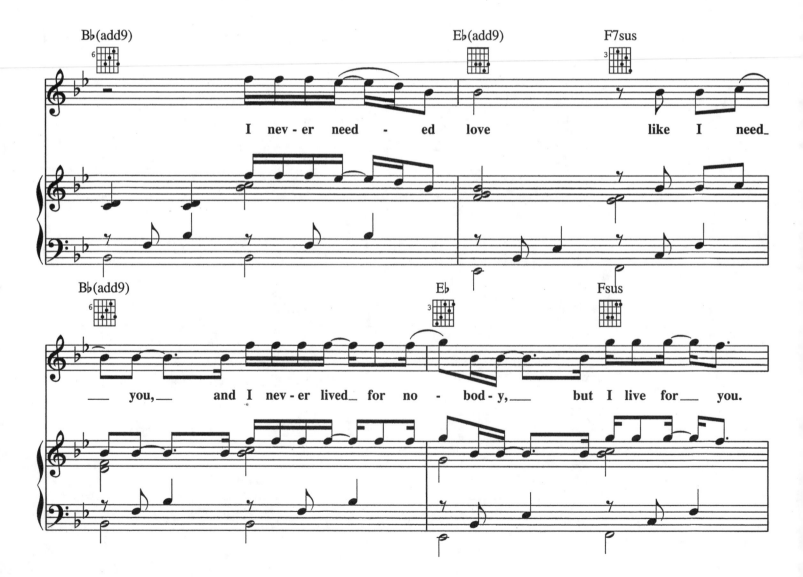

I nev-er need-ed love like I need_ _ you,_ and I nev-er lived_ for no-bod-y,_ but I live for_ you.

with you. _____

When I'm ___ with you. _____

# WHITHER THOU GOEST

Words and Music by
GUY SINGER

# WITH THIS RING

Words and Music by
CLYDE OTIS and VINCENT CORSO

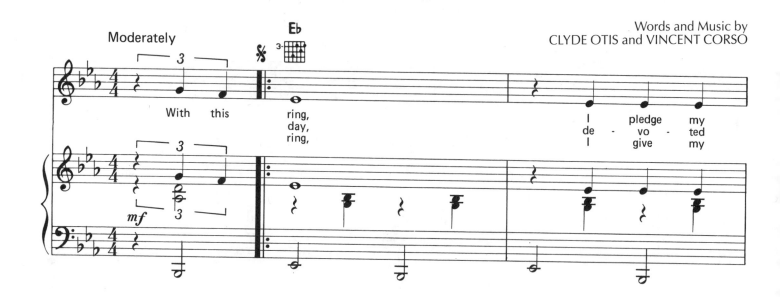

With this ring,
day,
ring,
I pledge my
de - vo - ted
I give my

love to you, _____ I vow a heart that's true. _____ With this
I will be _____ now and a
all to you, _____ now and my whole life through,

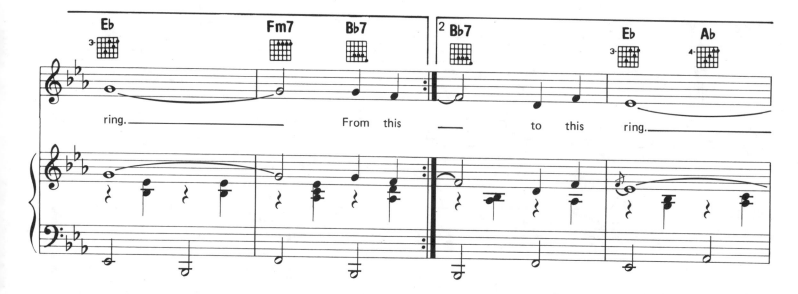

ring. _____ From this _____ to this ring. _____

# YOU DECORATED MY LIFE

Words and Music by
DEBBIE HUPP and BOB MORRISON

All my life was a pa - per
rhyme with no rea - son

once plain, pure and white;
in an un - fin - ished song;

Till you moved with your pen
There was no har - mo - ny

chang - in' moods now and then
life meant noth - in' to me,

till the
un - til

bal - ance was right.
you came a - long.

Then you add - ed some mu - sic,
And you brought out the col - ors,

And you_____ dec-o-ra-ted my life

by paint-in' your love_____ all o-ver my heart,_

You dec-o-ra-ted my_ life._____

Like a

# YOU NEEDED ME

Words and Music by
RANDY GOODRUM

Moderately

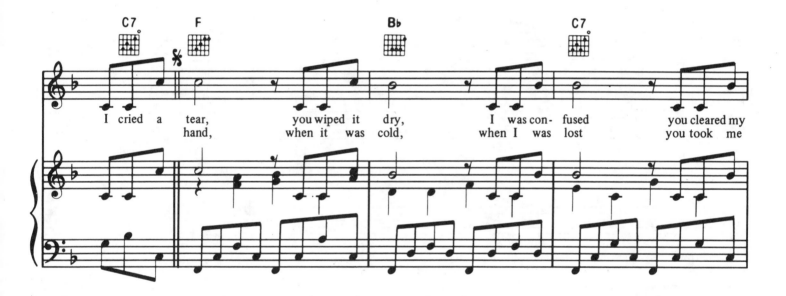

I cried a tear, you wiped it dry, I was con- fused you cleared my
hand, when it was cold, when I was lost you took me

mind, I sold my soul, you bought it back for me __ and held me
home You gave me hope, when I was at the end __ and turned my

# YOU'RE MY EVERYTHING

J. M. DE SCARANO, N. SKORSKY and L. GOMEZ

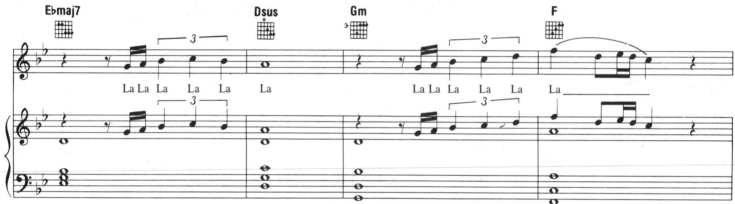

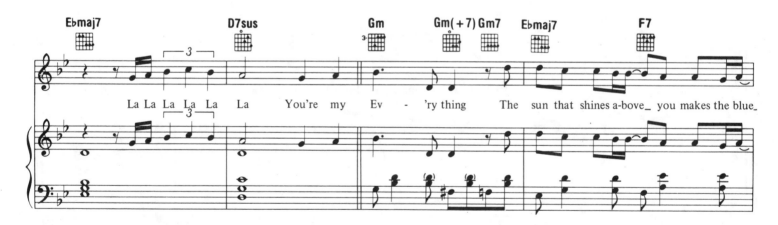

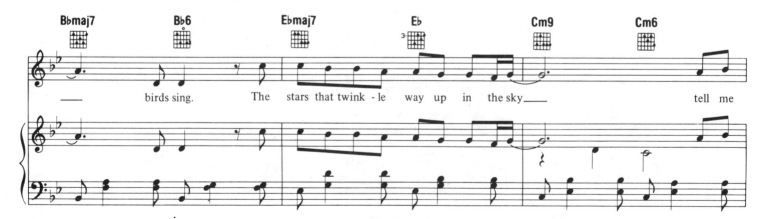

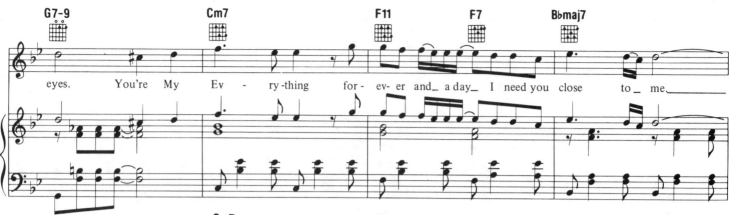

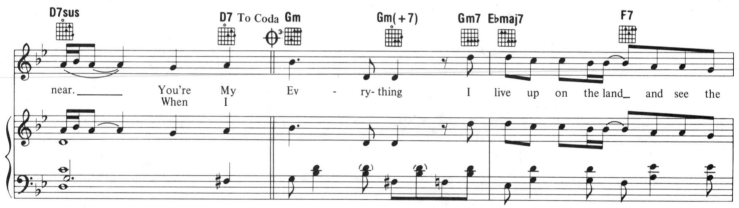

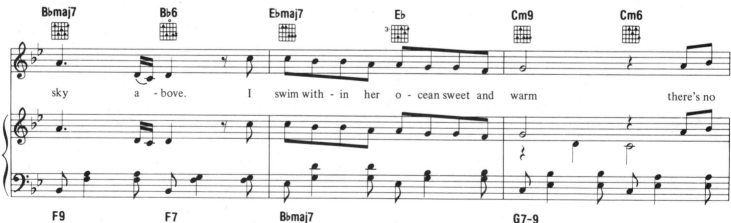

# YOU'LL NEVER WALK ALONE

### (From "CAROUSEL")

Lyrics by OSCAR HAMMERSTEIN II
Music by RICHARD RODGERS

Moderately

*(with great warmth, like a hymn)*

**When you walk through a storm, hold your head up high And don't be a-fraid of the dark, At the end of the storm is a**

# THE GREATEST SONGS EVER WRITTEN

### Arranged for Piano, Voice & Guitar

## 150 OF THE MOST BEAUTIFUL SONGS EVER

Over 400 pages of slow and sentimental ballads, including: Come In From The Rain • Edelweiss • The First Time Ever I Saw Your Face • For All We Know • How Deep Is Your Love • I Have Dreamed • I'll Be Seeing You • If We Only Have Love • Love Is Blue • Red Roses For A Blue Lady • Songbird • Summertime • Unchained Melody • Yesterday, When I Was Young • Young At Heart • many more.
____00360735 .........................$19.95

## THE BEST LOVE SONGS EVER
**Newly revised!**
A collection of 66 favorite love songs, including: The Anniversary Song • (They Long To Be) Close To You • Endless Love • Here and Now • Just The Way You Are • Longer • Love Takes Time • Misty • My Funny Valentine • So In Love • You Needed Me • Your Song.
____00359198 .........................$15.95

## THE BEST BIG BAND SONGS EVER
**Newly revised!**
69 of the greatest big band songs ever, including: Ballin' The Jack • Basin Street Blues • Boogie Woogie Bugle Boy • The Continental • Don't Get Around Much Anymore • In The Mood • Let A Smile Be Your Umbrella • Marie • Moonglow • Opus One • Satin Doll • Sentimental Journey • String Of Pearls • Who's Sorry Now.
____00359129 .........................$15.95

## THE BEST CHRISTMAS SONGS EVER
**Newly revised!**
A collection of 72 of the most-loved songs of the season, including: Blue Christmas • The Chipmunk Song • Frosty The Snow Man • A Holly Jolly Christmas • Home For The Holidays • I'll Be Home For Christmas • Jingle-Bell Rock • Let It Snow! Let It Snow! Let It Snow ! • Parade Of The Wooden Soldiers • Rudolph The Red-Nosed Reindeer • Suzy Snowflake • Toyland • Up On The House-Top • What Child Is This?
____00359130 .........................$15.95

## THE BEST ROCK SONGS EVER

70 of the best rock songs from yesterday & today, including: All Day And All Of The Night • All Shook Up • Ballroom Blitz • Bennie And The Jets • Blue Suede Shoes • Born To Be Wild • Boys Are Back In Town • Every Breath You Take • Faith • Free Bird • Hey Jude • I Still Haven't Found What I'm Looking For • Livin' On A Prayer • Lola • Louie Louie • Maggie May • Money • (She's) Some Kind Of Wonderful • Takin' Care Of Business • Walk This Way • We Didn't Start The Fire • We Got The Beat • Wild Thing • more!
____00490424 .........................$14.95

## THE BEST COUNTRY SONGS EVER
**Newly revised!**
We've updated this outstanding collection of country songs to include even more of your favorites — over 65 in all! Featuring: Always On My Mind • Behind Closed Doors • Could I Have This Dance • Crazy • Daddy Sang Bass • D-I-V-O-R-C-E • Forever And Ever, Amen • God Bless The U.S.A. • Grandpa (Tell Me 'Bout The Good Old Days) • Help Me Make It Through The Night • I Fall To Pieces • If We Make It Through December • Jambalaya (On The Bayou) • Love Without End, Amen • Mammas Don't Let Your Babies Grow Up To Be Cowboys • Stand By Your Man • Through The Years • and more.
____00359135 .........................$15.95

## THE BEST STANDARDS EVER
**Newly Revised!**
### Volume 1 (A-L)
72 beautiful ballads, including: All The Things You Are • Bewitched • Can't Help Lovin' Dat Man • Don't Get Around Much Anymore • Getting To Know You • God Bless' The Child • Hello, Young Lovers • I Got It Bad And That Ain't Good • It's Only A Paper Moon • I've Got You Under My Skin • The Lady Is A Tramp • Little White Lies.
____00359231 .........................$15.95

### Volume 2 (M-Z)
72 songs, including: Makin' Whoopee • Misty • Moonlight In Vermont • My Funny Valentine • Old Devil Moon • The Party's Over • People Will Say We're In Love • Smoke Gets In Your Eyes • Strangers In The Night • Tuxedo Junction • Yesterday.
____00359232 .........................$15.95

## THE BEST EASY LISTENING SONGS EVER
**Newly revised!**
A collection of 75 mellow favorites, featuring: All Out Of Love • Can't Smile Without You • (They Long To Be) Close To You • Every Breath You Take • Eye In The Sky • How Am I Supposed To Live Without You • I Dreamed A Dream • Imagine • Love Takes Time • Piano Man • The Rainbow Connection • Sing • Vision Of Love • Your Song.
____00359193 .........................$15.95

## THE BEST SONGS EVER!
**Newly revised!**
This prestigious collection has just been updated and revised to include even more recent "contemporary classics" — 76 songs in all, featuring: All I Ask Of You • Cabaret • Can't Smile Without You • Candle In The Wind • Do-Re-Mi • Don't Know Much • Feelings • Fly Me To The Moon • The Girl From Ipanema • Here's That Rainy Day • I Can't Help Falling In Love • I Left My Heart In San Francisco • I Write The Songs • Imagine • In The Mood • Let it Be Me • Longer • Love On The Rocks • More • My Way • People • Send In The Clowns • Some Enchanted Evening • Somewhere Out There • Stormy Weather • Strangers In The Night • Sunrise, Sunset • What A Wonderful World.
____00359224 .........................$17.95

## THE BEST BROADWAY SONGS EVER
**Newly revised!**
We've made this book even better with the addition of songs from some of Broadway's latest blockbusters such as Phantom Of The Opera, Les Miserables, Miss Saigon, and Aspects Of Love — over 65 songs in all! Highlights include: All I Ask Of You • As Long As He Needs Me • Bess, You Is My Woman • Bewitched • Camelot • Climb Ev'ry Mountain • Comedy Tonight • Don't Cry For Me Argentina • Everything's Coming Up Roses • Getting To Know You • I Could Have Danced All Night • I Dreamed A Dream • If I Were A Rich Man • The Last Night Of The World • Love Changes Everything • Oklahoma! • Ol' Man River • People • Try To Remember • and many, many more!
____00309155 .........................$15.95

**Hal Leonard Publishing Corporation**
7777 West Bluemound Road P.O. Box 13819 Milwaukee, WI 53213

0192